Focus on Learning Technologies

Focus on Learning Technologies

Nicky Hockly

OXFORD
UNIVERSITY PRESS

OXFORD
UNIVERSITY PRESS

ISBN: 978 0 19 400311 7

Printed in China

This book is printed on paper from certified and well-managed sources

ACKNOWLEDGEMENTS

*The authors and publisher are grateful to those who have given permission to reproduce
the following extracts and adaptations of copyright material:* p.18 Extract from
Foreword (page i) by Professor John Sinclair in *Collins COBUILD English Course* by
Jane Willis and Dave Willis. Published by Collins COBUILD, 1988. Reproduced
by permission of Jane Willis. p.42 Figure 2.1 'Framework of Digital Literacies'
from page 6 (Table 1.1) of *Digital Literacies* by Gavin Dudeney, Nicky Hockly
and Mark Pegrum © 2013 by Routledge. Reproduced by permission of Taylor
and Francis Books UK. pp.44–45 Extract from "Coding for Kids: The New
Vocational Education" by Larry Cuban, www.larrycuban.wordpress.com,
19 May 2015. Reproduced by permission of Larry Cuban. p.50 Extract
from "Children's perceptions of learning with an interactive whiteboard"
by Lorena Yáñez and Yvette Coyle, *ELT Journal* Vol. 65 (4), 2011: 448–452.
Reproduced by permission of Oxford University Press. p.68 Adapted
extract from *"The safe use of new technologies"* by The Office for Standards in
Education, Children's Services and Skills (Ofsted), February 2010 included
within *"Do we have safer children in a digital world? A review of progress since
the 2008 Byron Review"* by Professor Tanya Byron © Crown Copyright 2010.
Contains public sector information licensed under the Open Government
Licence v3.0 http://www.nationalarchives.gov.uk/doc/open-government-
licence/version/3. p.79 Extract from *Contemporary Computer-Assisted Language
Learning* © Michael Thomas, Hayo Reinders and Mark Warschauer and
Contributors, 2013. Reproduced by permission of Bloomsbury Academic,
an imprint of Bloomsbury Publishing Plc. p.100 Extract from "The Rise of
K–12 Blended Learning" by Michael B. Horn and Heather Staker © January
2011 by Innosight Institute, Inc. Reproduced by permission of The Clayton
Christensen Institute. p.109 Extract from "EFL learners' reading on mobile
phones" by Lo-Li Huang and Chih-Cheng Lin, *The JALT CALL Journal*, Vol. 7 (1),
2011. Reproduced by permission of The JALT CALL Journal. p.119 Extracts
from "Interactive Language Learning through Speech-Enabled Virtual
Scenarios", by Hazel Morton, Nancie Gunson, and Mervyn Jack, *Advances
in Human-Computer Interaction*, vol. 2012, Article ID 389523, 14 pages, 2012.
doi:10.1155/2012/389523 © Hazel Morton et al. Released under the Creative
Commons Attribution License http://creativecommons.org/licenses/by/3.0/.

To my mother.

For her constant encouragement of my reading—and writing—from a very early age.

Contents

Contents

Acknowledgments

This book attempts to condense and summarize a wide variety of CALL (Computer-Assisted Language Learning) research carried out by professional researchers, and by classroom teachers with their students, in a relatively short volume. Given the constraints of space, not everyone who has contributed to this lively and growing field appears in the pages of this book. Nevertheless, I would like to thank all of those—researchers and teachers, named and unnamed—on whose work this book is based. Without your methodical, questioning, and frequently critical stances, the field of educational technology would be a poorer one. And, of course, a special thank you must go to the countless language students who have frequently been at the receiving end of educational technology, both when it is effective, and when it is not.

I would also like to thank the series editors, Patsy Lightbown and Nina Spada, whose encouragement and consistently positive feedback made writing this book a thoroughly enjoyable task. Ditto to OUP editor Julia Bell and copy-editor Alex Paramour. You were all a delight to work with.

Finally, a heartfelt thank you to my colleague, co-author, and co-director at The Consultants-E, Gavin Dudeney, for his constant encouragement and belief in me as a writer and professional, which now spans almost two decades.

Series Editors' Preface

The Oxford Key Concepts for the Language Classroom series is designed to provide accessible information about research on topics that are important to second language teachers. Each volume focuses on a particular area of second/foreign-language learning and teaching, covering both background research and classroom-based studies. The emphasis is on how knowing about this research can guide teachers in their instructional planning, pedagogical activities, and assessment of learners' progress.

The idea for the series was inspired by the book *How Languages are Learned*. Many colleagues have told us that they appreciate the way that book can be used either as part of a university teacher education program or in a professional development course for experienced teachers. They have commented on the value of publications that show teachers and future teachers how knowing about research on language learning and teaching can help them think about their own teaching principles and practices.

This series is oriented to the educational needs and abilities of school-aged children (5–18 years old), with distinct chapters focusing on research that is specific to primary- and secondary-level learners. The volumes are written for second language teachers, whether their students are minority language speakers learning the majority language or students learning a foreign language in a classroom far from the communities where the language is spoken. Some of the volumes will be useful to 'mainstream' teachers who have second language learners among their students, but have limited training in second/foreign language teaching. Some of the volumes will also be primarily for teachers of English, whereas others will be of interest to teachers of other languages as well.

The series includes volumes on topics that are key for second language teachers of school-aged children, and each volume is written by authors whose research and teaching experience have focused on learners and teachers in this age group. While much has been written about some of these topics, most publications are either 'how to' methodology texts with no explicit link to research, or academic works that are designed for researchers and postgraduate students who require a thorough scholarly treatment of the research, rather than an overview and interpretation for classroom practice. Instructors in programs for teachers often find that the methodology texts lack the academic background appropriate for a university course and that the scholarly works are too long, too difficult, or not sufficiently classroom-oriented for the needs of teachers and future teachers. The volumes in this series are intended to bridge that gap.

The books are enriched by the inclusion of *Spotlight Studies* that represent important research and *Classroom Snapshots* that provide concrete examples of teaching/learning events in the second language classroom. In addition, through a variety of activities, readers will be able to integrate this information with their own experiences of learning and teaching.

Introduction

Although learning technologies are not found in every classroom in the world, they are becoming increasingly common in classrooms in both developed and developing countries. Many believe that, where possible, children in primary and secondary schools should have access to technologies that can help them learn. Many also believe that children should develop the digital skills that will ensure that they can participate fully as responsible citizens in our increasingly digital and globalized world. As we will see in this book, these beliefs have affected government policies and curricula the world over. Indeed, the implementation of learning technologies in schools is as much a political and economic issue as it is an educational one.

The aim of this book is to examine how learning technologies have been used in primary and secondary schools in a variety of settings, and to consider to what extent they can affect language learning outcomes. The book will be of interest to educators who are new to learning technologies, and also to experienced teachers who may be using technologies regularly in their classrooms and are interested in exploring what the research has to say about them.

Chapter 1 provides an overview of learning technologies: what they are, how they have been used over the past 30-odd years in language teaching, and how primary and secondary school students use digital technologies in their everyday lives as well as at school.

In Chapter 2, we examine the concepts of 21st-century skills and digital literacies that appear in many curricula in primary and secondary schools. We also discuss how national educational policies affect the implementation of learning technologies in schools, and what the research has to say about this.

In Chapters 3 and 4, we explore research that has been carried out with primary and secondary school learners in both foreign language and second language contexts. In Chapter 3, our focus is on young learners from pre-kindergarten through about age 11. In Chapter 4, our focus is on adolescents aged approximately 12 to 18 years old. In each of these chapters, we first identify some of the factors that affect how young learners and adolescents use technologies. We then focus on the language classroom and look in detail at a range of research studies in an attempt to gauge to what extent learning technologies may help primary and secondary school students learn a second or foreign language. Chapter 5 will provide a summary of the most important points covered in detail in the earlier chapters.

Some of the studies we review will be designated as *Spotlight Studies*. These studies illustrate the broad range of approaches that are used in researching the effectiveness of learning technologies in supporting language learning. Some are large-scale studies involving thousands of students in many countries; some are small-scale studies involving single classrooms and small groups of students. Together, these studies reflect the wide range of issues that have concerned researchers in this field. Also included in this book are *Classroom Snapshots*, brief descriptions of how learning technologies are used in practice by teachers and students. They provide concrete examples of how teachers and learners deploy learning technologies both inside and outside the classroom, and they allow us to connect our discussion of general principles to moments in real classrooms. In addition, each chapter will include some *Activities* that invite you to deepen your understanding of underlying questions, assumptions, or research findings through personal reflection, evaluating research, or doing some research of your own.

An annotated list of Suggestions for Further Reading will provide the interested reader with a range of resources to explore further. The Glossary provides definitions of terms that may be unfamiliar to some readers. These terms will be in bold print the first time they appear in the text, and the Index will allow you to find other mentions of them. The References section will provide complete information for all the sources that are cited in the chapters.

The appearance of digital technologies in the language classroom may feel like a recent development. In fact, technology has been around for over 30 years in English language teaching, and it has generated a considerable amount of research. It is this rich research tradition, as well as more recent developments, that we will explore in this book, as we examine the effects that digital technologies have had on English language teaching and learning to date.

1

Learning Technologies in Language Teaching

Preview

Ask any group of teachers how they feel about using technology in the classroom, and responses will range from enthusiastic, through reluctant, to downright fearful. This reflects attitudes to technology in society as a whole. We are simultaneously enamored and suspicious of our technological gadgets of the present, and hopeful and fearful about the technological developments of the future. We feel we cannot live without our cell phones but are worried about how always being connected affects our social relationships. We admire advances in technology that make our lives easier but fear a future controlled by machines.

Indeed, it is difficult to separate the use of technology in education from its role in wider society. In language teaching, learning technologies are closely tied to wider economic, social, and political interests. To think otherwise is naive. In the words of Neil Selwyn:

> educational technology needs to be understood as a profoundly political affair – a site of constant conflict and struggle between different interests and groups.

> (Selwyn, 2014, p. vii)

Simply put, when we consider—and investigate—the uses of learning technologies in the language classroom, we need to keep in mind a wider range of factors than may be necessary when researching other areas. And, as we shall see, it is this that makes research into learning technologies particularly challenging.

What Are Learning Technologies?

Technology has been used in language teaching for a very long time. Indeed, if one defines technology simply as 'a tool to help us get things done', it can be argued that the copybook, blackboard, and pen are forms of technology that have enhanced teaching and learning for centuries. However, in this book we will be looking at *digital learning technologies*—in other words, the technologies that first made their appearance in language education in the early 1980s, with the advent of computer software for language learning.

First, what do we mean by 'learning technologies'? We are not simply referring to computers and related hardware such as printers and projectors but also to programs and tools—the software. And, perhaps most importantly, we need to consider how teachers and learners—who we might call the 'liveware' (Hockly & Clandfield, 2010)—interact with these technologies and each other, and how this relates to language learning.

Examples of hardware and software we typically see in language classrooms are presented in Table 1.1. We explore in later chapters how some of these tools have been used and researched in language teaching, and the Glossary provides definitions of those tools that may be unfamiliar to you.

Language learning hardware	computers, such as PCs and laptops mobile devices, such as **cell phones** and **tablets** **interactive whiteboards (IWBs)**, digital cameras audio recorders **MP3** and **MP4 players** **e-readers** **videoconferencing equipment** **games consoles**
Language learning software	programs (for example, for grammar or vocabulary practice; see Classroom Snapshot 1.1) **blogs** **wikis** **podcasts** **virtual learning environments (VLEs)** **learning management systems (LMSs)**

Table 1.1 Hardware and software typically found in language classrooms

However, as suggested above, what we are most interested in is the 'liveware' (the learners and teachers): their interactions with technology and each other, and how this affects language learning. After all, there is not much point in using often expensive technologies in the classroom if they are not positively affecting learning processes and outcomes. This, then, is the issue that forms the main focus of the book: what does the research tell us about how, or indeed *if*, learning technologies support and enhance language learning at both primary and secondary school level?

What's in a Name?

I use the term 'learning technologies' in this book to refer to any digital technology that can be used in the language classroom to support student learning. This is not the only term I could use, but it is one of the most general terms currently available, and given that I will be examining research across a range of contexts, I feel that it is more suited to our purposes than some of the other terms used in the field. Probably the most common of these alternatives is 'CALL' (Computer-Assisted Language Learning), a term coined in the 1980s and still much used, particularly in research circles. Less commonly used, and now rather old-fashioned, is 'CBI' (Computer-Based Instruction). Both CALL and CBI are acronyms that go back to early uses of computers in language teaching.

The term CALL has generated much debate over the years (Levy & Hubbard, 2005). On the plus side, it has a very strong research tradition and reflects a continued belief in the computer—or what we might now more accurately call 'technology'—as the key mediating factor in this type of learning. There is a perfectly reasonable case for the continued use of the term CALL in our field, based precisely on its strong research tradition, its ongoing concern with many central issues over the years, and the wide range of technology- and language-learning-related topics it covers (Levy, 2013).

On the minus side, with the rise of learning via mobile devices the emphasis on 'computer' in this term is starting to feel decidedly dated; indeed, some researchers argue that the term is now obsolete, as learning with technologies no longer takes place only via computers in formal learning contexts (Jarvis & Krashen, 2014). As Levy and Hubbard point out, like much of the terminology involved in English language teaching (ELT), the term CALL has been the site of 'a struggle for dominance and recognition' (2005, p. 144). For instance, CALL as a label for the field may have more traction in university settings because of its association with the term 'computer' in departments of computer science and computer engineering. There, the concept of 'computer' encompasses the full range of digital devices and the networks that connect them, as well as the great variety of software, including mobile **apps** (Hubbard, personal communication, 7 October 2015). In short, CALL is a term that can appear rather abstract to classroom teachers, who frequently prefer more descriptive terms such as 'learning technologies'.

The feeling that CALL may need to be replaced by a more modern-sounding alternative resulted in terms such as 'Technology Enhanced Language Learning' (TELL), which also dates back to the 1980s, although it never became as widespread as CALL. In 2000, Kern and Warschauer made a case for the term 'network-based language teaching' (NBLT), which they felt de-emphasized the computer-program-based learning reflected in the older term CALL and emphasized the new opportunities for human-to-human communication via networks facilitated by technology; however, this term was not widely taken up either.

Terms that have been in vogue more recently include 'educational technologies' (or 'edtech') and the more generic 'Information and Communications Technology' (ICT). Other terms you may come across in relation to the use of technologies in education are 'Computer-Mediated Communication' (CMC)—another one from the 1980s—and, more recently, terms used to refer to mobile learning in our field: 'Mobile-Assisted Language Learning' (MALL), a term clearly derived from CALL, and 'Mobile-Assisted Language in Use' (MALU) (Jarvis & Achilleos, 2003). Nevertheless, the term CALL is still widely respected and used, and it is likely to be with us for some time to come. For this reason, although we use the generic term 'learning technologies' throughout this volume, we will also use the term CALL at points, particularly when it has been used by researchers and theorists in very specific ways (see, for example, 'The History of Technology in ELT' on page 14, and the sections on research in Chapter 2).

What Do You Think about Learning Technologies?

Before we look in depth at how digital technologies have been used in language learning and at what the research has to say about this, let us pause for a moment for you to reflect on your own attitudes to learning technologies and how you think they relate to language learning (see Activity 1.1).

Once you have reflected on what you think about these statements, ask other teachers what their reactions are. Ask teachers of different subjects and teachers who work with children of different ages. Ask teachers who work with native speakers and with **second language** (**L2**) learners. Do they agree? What are the points of greatest disagreement? What do you think the reasons might be for these differences? Summarize your findings and refer to your notes from time to time as you read this volume. We will return to these statements in Chapter 5.

Activity 1.1

The statements below represent views that some teachers hold about learning technologies in the language classroom. Read each statement and check one of the columns to indicate how much you agree or disagree with it.

SA = Strongly Agree   A = Agree   D = Disagree   SD = Strongly Disagree

Statement	Your response			
1 If teachers use technology with young learners, they need to pay attention to issues like e-safety.	SA	A	D	SD
2 Tools like blogs and wikis can help students improve their writing skills.				
3 Teachers need training to be able to use technology effectively with students.				
4 Governments should provide funding to schools to buy the latest educational technologies.				
5 Technology depersonalizes learning.				
6 Learners communicate only with machines and not with each other if they are using technology in the classroom.				
7 Technology games, such as vocabulary or grammar games, can improve learning outcomes.				
8 Technology can effectively support students with special educational needs.				
9 Young learners and adolescents are naturally good at using new technologies.				
10 Technologies like cell phones should be kept out of the language classroom as they don't teach, they distract.				

How Are Learning Technologies Used in Language Teaching?

Let us now turn to what actually happens in the language classroom and examine three examples of how learning technologies can be used to teach English. Learners of primary school age and of secondary school age have very different needs and characteristics; even within these two age groups, there are important differences. This relates to all areas of schooling and, of course, also to the use of technology within education. We will examine these differences and how they relate to educational technology in more depth in Chapters 3 and 4, but for the moment, our Classroom Snapshots are all from primary school classrooms to provide some consistency to our examples.

Read Classroom Snapshots 1.1, 1.2, and 1.3. Each describes a scenario where primary school students are working with digital technology in the language or literacy classroom. Think about the differences and similarities.

- Are the students working individually or in groups?
- Who are they communicating with: each other, the teacher, and/or a computer?
- Are they comprehending or producing language?
- Is the activity part of a long-term project or is it a 'one-off' event?
- What role does the technology play in the activity?
- What role does the teacher play?
- What theories of language learning underpin the digital materials and the teaching approach?
- How much control or choice do the learners have over the learning material, and how do they interact with the material?
- How does the technology support or enhance their learning?

Classroom Snapshot 1.1

Young learners studying **English as a Foreign Language** (**EFL**) in Japan are sitting individually at computer terminals. They are playing a game that prepares them for a national standardized multiple-choice English-language proficiency test in Japan called *Jidō Eiken*. They have a choice of six different games, and the learners are each playing the game of their choice. These are the six games:

- A game in which animated mallets with English words pop up from holes. The child needs to listen to a word and click on the right mallet as quickly as possible.
- A game with three pictures moving around the screen. The child needs to listen and then click on the picture that matches an oral description.
- A game in which the child listens to an oral description and identifies the matching picture. Then the pictures are covered and moved around the screen, and the child needs to click on the correct picture again.
- A card game in which the child plays against the computer, listening to English words and 'collecting' the matching cards as quickly as possible.
- A car racing game in which the child answers English-language questions and gets more fuel for every correct answer.
- A card memory game in which the child is given oral clues and needs to memorize where the matching cards are located on the screen.

(Goto Butler, Someya, & Fukuhara, 2014)

Classroom Snapshot 1.2

Young EFL learners are sitting at desks in a rural school in Uruguay. Each child is sitting in front of a small low-cost laptop computer provided by the school. The school has no qualified English teachers, and the learners are looking at a large screen at the front of the class, where a qualified English instructor, who lives in Argentina, is delivering a lesson to them via videoconference. This 'remote' teacher shows the children pictures of new vocabulary, drills the pronunciation, asks questions, gets them to practice the words in pairs, and then asks them to type the new vocabulary into their laptops. The Uruguayan classroom teacher is helping by managing the class. For example, she nominates learners to answer the remote teacher's questions, puts the learners in pairs to practice, translates new words into Spanish for the learners if necessary, and checks they are typing the new words correctly into their laptops. This English lesson is one of many taking place throughout Uruguay and is part of the country's One Laptop Per Child (OLPC) initiative, called *Plan Ceibal*. *Ceibal* stands for 'Basic Informatic Educative Connectivity for Online Learning' (*Conectividad Educativa de Informática Básica para el Aprendizaje en Línea*), and also refers obliquely to the indigenous *ceibo* tree.

Classroom Snapshot 1.3

Fifth-grade students in the USA are listening to their teacher read a chapter from a book. Two-thirds of the students in the class are **English Language Learners (ELLs)**; in other words, English is not their **first language (L1)**. The students all have laptop computers and are live-blogging their thoughts and comments while listening to the teacher read aloud. The teacher pauses regularly to give the students time to blog. During these pauses, students can read each other's comments as they are posted and respond to them. At the end of the class, all the posts are automatically saved to the class blog. Sessions like this take place twice a week for 20 minutes, and students either listen to the teacher reading a chapter from a book or watch a video together, with pauses for live-blogging. The project has been going for eight months.

(Zheng & Warschauer, 2015) ▓

What the Snapshots Tell Us

These three Classroom Snapshots are all of primary school students, but they show very different contexts. The first two snapshots show learners of English in EFL contexts in Japan and Uruguay. The third shows native English-speaking students working with ELLs in a mainstream schooling context in the USA. Clearly, the amount of exposure to English that the learners receive in these contexts differs significantly. EFL learners typically receive a few hours of language instruction a week and have little or no contact with English outside the classroom. ELLs in schools where their classmates are native speakers of English may receive targeted language instruction, but they are also exposed to English outside the classroom, if not necessarily in the home. ELLs usually have most of the school curriculum delivered in English. (For more on the teaching of language and content, see Lightbown, 2014, and de Oliveira & Schleppegrell, 2015, in this series.)

Apart from differing in their geographical locations and language learning contexts, these learners also have access to different learning technologies and learning materials with widely differing aims. The design of these materials affects the way students work (individually or in pairs/groups); who they communicate with (the computer, a remote teacher, and/or each other); the language they work with (for example, vocabulary and/or grammar); the language skills they use (reading, writing, listening, and/or speaking); and whether they are working with language for comprehension and/or for production.

In Classroom Snapshot 1.1, the learners work individually and interact with computers, playing games that require them to recognize words and phrases, but they do not need to produce language. The students can play these games during class time, or at home if they have access to computers, and this can be programmed as an intensive activity within the language curriculum in the run-up to the *Jidō Eiken* test. The teacher does not need to mediate the activity and, indeed, does not even need to be present. The learners use the receptive skills of reading and listening to play these games: they read individual words and/or listen to words and phrases. The content of the games is adapted to their level of language proficiency, and the learners have an element of choice over which of six games they choose to play and how often they play them. The technology—games on a computer—is the main component of this learning experience for the learners.

The learning theory that underpins these materials is mainly behaviorist in orientation, with a strong focus on recognizing and memorizing language. Some principles of game mechanics in evidence. The game technology used here may increase the learners' motivation, but according to research that investigated it, playing these games did not necessarily translate into improved test scores for these students. The researchers suggest that the skills needed to achieve high scores in some of these games, such as short-term memory skills, were not tested in the *Jidō Eiken* test; in addition, they suggest 'it is also possible that over-attractiveness, or over-excitement, hinders learning' for these primary-level students (Goto Butler et al., 2014, p. 274). What is also interesting about these types of computer-based games from a pedagogical perspective is that they are often called 'interactive' games: the children interact with other players—really controlled by the computer—and they interact with elements on the screen by clicking or moving them. However, when we consider interaction from the perspective of learning a language, we tend to understand something different. 'Interaction' in second language acquisition terms usually refers both to understanding and processing language and to *producing* it—in either spoken or written form—for meaningful communication (see Oliver & Philp, 2015, in this series).

In Classroom Snapshot 1.2, the EFL learners are using technology to work in a very different manner. In many ways, this is a standard EFL class focusing on the learning of new vocabulary. The major difference is that the language teacher is not physically present in the classroom but is 'beamed in' from another location. In this instance, the videoconferencing technology is the *medium* through which the class is delivered, but the learning materials and the learning experience for the students conform to what we might consider standard **communicative language teaching** (CLT). The role of the remote teacher is central in this particular lesson: she presents new words, provides a model of pronunciation, and ensures that the learners are given time to practice in pairs. The classroom teacher is equally important as the facilitator 'on the ground'. The learners communicate both with teachers and with each other, and the technology is almost incidental to the class—at least in *language learning* terms. Of course, on another level, the technology is crucial to the whole enterprise. Without trained remote teachers delivering English lessons via videoconferencing, many students in rural primary schools in Uruguay would have no access to English whatsoever. These *Ceibal en Inglés* remote lessons form part of a long-term national strategy to increase English language provision in the country, so the project receives government funding and support. We revisit the *Ceibal en Inglés* project in Chapter 3.

In Classroom Snapshot 1.3, we have an **English as a Second Language** (ESL) context, where ELLs are working together with native-speaker children in a literacy class that is not specifically focused on second language learning but rather requires listening to, understanding, and engaging with a text. The children are using an online blogging platform to communicate their thoughts and reactions with each other while the teacher is reading it aloud. This means that they are processing—recognizing and comprehending—the language they hear, and then producing their own language—expressing their own thoughts—in response while the teacher pauses. In this case, although the role of the teacher is central in reading the text, the children are being given a 'voice' at the same time and are encouraged to engage with, reflect on, and respond to the content they hear.

Here we see technology being used as a tool to support what might be considered a traditional reading aloud/storytelling class. The technology *facilitates* and *enhances* the activity in that students are provided with a digital 'backchannel' in which to communicate about the text, and the digital medium means that their contributions can be saved automatically and added to a class blog at the end of the 20-minute lesson. In addition, the choice of tool here, a live-blogging platform, specifically allows for written interaction and communication among students. Over time, a bank of their contributions is built up on the class blog, providing a useful record of how individual students' writing—and thinking—skills develop during the eight months of the project. The researchers note that although the ELLs' participation in the activity was dependent on their language ability, cultural knowledge, and, for a few, familiarity with the technology, there were significant gains in the fluency and complexity of the learners' writing over the course of the project.

Factors Affecting Technology Use in Language Classrooms

The point of providing these three snapshots is not to suggest that any one is 'better' than another. They are simply *different*. Each snapshot responds to a whole range of contextual, social, political, and pedagogical factors such as those below, which, in any context, will affect how learning technologies are used:

- whether the learners are working in an EFL, **CBLT** (**Content-based Language Teaching**), or mainstream schooling environment
- whether the learners are of primary school or secondary school age, and related to this, their stage of cognitive and motor skills development
- whether the learners are working in a 'resource-rich'—or 'high-tech'—environment where there is plenty of reliable access to technology, or in a low-resource—or 'low-tech'—environment where the learners have little, unreliable, or no access to digital learning technologies

- whether the use of specific learning technologies is part of a long-term government educational policy and is supported by funds for hardware such as laptops, for the development of learning materials, and, crucially, for teacher training
- whether the digital learning materials are created for a specific outcome, such as providing practice materials for a national language proficiency exam, or whether the learners create their own digital products to practice or showcase their language skills
- whether the learners are using tools that allow for interaction and collaboration, and whether the design of learning materials and tasks supports this
- whether the tools are essential to the learning experience or outcomes, or whether the tools play a supporting or facilitating role and could even be replaced by traditional tools like pen and paper
- what ideas about language learning underpin the design of the materials and how these are delivered—for example, whether learners are expected to comprehend or produce language while working with the digital materials, and whether they work alone or with others.

These are some of the factors that affect the use of learning technologies in language education and that are illustrated in our three snapshots on pages 8–9. They are factors that will reappear in the research we examine later. Some are 'micro' factors that relate to the individual teacher, learners, and classroom. These might include teacher and learner—and, indeed, parent—attitudes to the use of technologies in language learning, access to technology in and out of class, access to—or lack of—teacher training and support, and the syllabus and/or coursebook. Some are 'macro' factors that relate to the wider context, for example the socioeconomic environment or government educational policies. Government policies in particular— frequently driven by political and economic considerations—can have profound effects on the use of educational technologies in the classroom. Even within a single country, such as the USA, differing policies at state level can dramatically affect the educational technology landscape. For example, as of the time of writing, Forsyth County in North Carolina has been leading the way in the integration of learners' own mobile devices in its public schools since 2008, thanks to a deliberate strategy of investment and teacher training. The city of New York, on the other hand, explicitly banned the use of cell phones in public schools in 2006, a ban lifted only in early 2015. This clearly has implications for what teachers and learners can or cannot do *legally* in the classroom, depending on where they are, even within the same country.

Activity 1.2

Think about the context in which you live, study, or teach. Make a list of the 'micro' factors that can affect the use of educational technologies in your context. Talk to local primary and secondary school teachers and students if you can to find out more about these. Also, make a list of the 'macro' factors that can affect the use of educational technologies in your context. Use the internet to research state-wide and/or country-wide government directives related to educational technologies. For example, use search phrases such as 'educational policy in [country]' or 'ICT in education'. You can also consult UNESCO's ICT in Education website, which can be helpful depending on where you are located.

The History of Technology in ELT

In the field of learning technologies for ELT, the use of computers is perhaps the area that has been most strongly influenced by industry developments in hardware and software. Of course, this makes perfect sense: the kinds of things computers could do directly influenced what sort of learning materials could be created. Although computers had been used in education previously, it was in the early 1980s that technology began to gain some traction in language teaching. Advances in computer hardware partly influenced this development, with cheaper personal computers and color monitors becoming available.

Below we take a closer look at how technology developments influenced English-language digital learning materials. It is important to understand the development of these materials as related to technology because they directly influenced what could—and could not—be done in the classroom and this, in turn, influenced CALL research studies. In the field of learning technologies, we cannot understand current research without understanding where it has come from and how it has been influenced by past developments.

The Development of CALL

The early era of computer-based language teaching runs from the mid-1980s to the mid-1990s. Initially limited to fill-in-the-blank and text-reconstruction activities, computers then developed multimedia capabilities, with images, sound, and even video. Educational CD-ROMs such as *Encarta* were produced, and English-language coursebooks slowly started to include multimedia CD-ROMs with additional self-study language practice for learners. The cassette-based language labs of the 1970s were replaced in some institutions—those with the necessary funds—with computer labs, rooms with banks of personal computers.

Warschauer (1996) and Warschauer and Healey (1998) described the development of early CALL in terms of three 'stages' which reflected contemporary paradigms of language learning. Bax (2003) critiqued the linear, chronological development suggested by Warschauer's 'stages' and instead suggested that CALL development reflected three different 'approaches'. Nevertheless, there is some overlap between the categorizations of Warschauer and Bax, and we briefly explore these below, along with the language learning theories that they reflect. (For a fuller treatment of language learning theories, approaches, and methods, see Lightbown & Spada, 2013; Richards & Rogers, 2014.)

Stage 1: 'Behavioristic' or 'Structural CALL' / 'Restricted CALL'

Computer-based language learning activities in this early stage of CALL development consisted of basic interactions and decontextualized exercises between the learner and computer, with minimal and unsophisticated automatic feedback given to the learner by the machine, for example 'correct'/'incorrect'. Activities—and feedback—were restricted to what could be programmed into the computer and were often based around short texts, with fill-in-the-blanks and text-reconstruction activities being the order of the day.

These kinds of activities, often referred to as **tutorial CALL**, reflect a *behaviorist* view of language as a formal system—of grammar, vocabulary, pronunciation, etc. The learner's task is to master each element in this system, in an incremental manner. The audiolingual method of using repetition drills and other practice activities with a focus on accuracy underlies many of the computer-based activities available at the time. Far from being an approach of simply historical interest, behaviorism still inspires plenty of educational technology materials available today. For example, several major ELT publishers offer online learning platforms in which learners can carry out accuracy-based grammar and vocabulary exercises with automatic feedback. There is also a wide range of mobile device apps that can help learners memorize vocabulary and grammatical structures. Some flashcard apps, for example, use algorithms based on a learner's previous performance in the app—known as **adaptive learning**—to determine what lexical items to show the learner, and how often. Clearly, there is a role for memorization and accuracy-/form-focused work in second language acquisition, and mobile apps can provide opportunities for this.

Stage 2: 'Communicative CALL' / 'Open CALL'

Both Communicative CALL (Warschauer, 1996) and Open CALL (Bax, 2003) allowed for more complex interactions between learner and computer, with more sophisticated feedback mechanisms providing the learners with more valuable information than simply 'correct'/'incorrect'. Technology could now assume a partial role as tutor, guiding learners to discover language rules and encouraging limited language production as well as recognition. Tasks could also now include writing, and more situated language practice within communicative activities.

These new kinds of activities reflected a *communicative* view of language— that is, language as a means for communication rather than as a formal system to be memorized. It also reflected a *cognitive* view of language, whereby learners are encouraged to think about language and construct their own incremental understanding of it. Learners could be encouraged to explore and experiment with language, and, most importantly, to use it to communicate in more open-ended interactions with computers and with other users, for example via email.

Stage 3: 'Integrative CALL' / 'Integrated CALL'

In this third stage, multimedia computer capabilities and early internet access translated into learning activities supported through images and sound—what Warschauer and Healey referred to as 'integrative CALL' and Bax as 'integrated CALL'. This, in turn, allowed learners to work with more language skills via the computer—primarily reading, writing, and listening. Research studies into the effect of multimedia materials on reading comprehension and vocabulary acquisition started to emerge in the early 1990s but were primarily focused on K–12 literacy classes, not on second language learning classes or students (see Reinking, 2005, for an overview of these studies). More recent studies have looked into EFL and ESL settings (see Chapter 4). Also, learners were increasingly able to communicate not just with machines but with each other via the computer, and it was around this time that the term 'Computer-Mediated Communication' (CMC), originally coined in the late 1970s, began to be used more widely to describe this new form of electronic communication in language learning (see page 6).

These new kinds of activities, like those in the previous stage, also reflect a *communicative* view of language, aligned to CLT. The increased opportunities for social interaction online and access to authentic materials also fit with **social constructivist** approaches and **situated learning**.

As we see from the three stages, or approaches, described above, the development of digital language learning materials—and research studies—were directly related to computer hardware and software capabilities of the time. They have also been influenced by the dominant learning theories of the time, particularly the move from audiolingualism to communicative language teaching.

Although Bax was writing of 'integrated CALL' in 2003, many of his observations still resonate today. For Bax, integrated CALL would be fully achieved when technology is integrated or 'normalized', becoming an inseparable part of our daily lives, including in the classroom. We certainly see digital devices such as cell phones becoming increasingly normalized, although not always in the language classroom. In terms of educational technology, the interactive whiteboard is arguably one of the first technologies to have become normalized—in some contexts. This is a technology that we will see more of in Chapter 2.

Walker and White (2013) have extended Warschauer and Bax's three-stage/approach model to reflect a 'move from computer-assisted language learning to "technology enhanced language learning" (TELL)', in which they see technology 'not as assisting language learning, but as part of the environment in which language exists and is used' (2013, p. 9). They point out that technology available these days includes mobile devices, as well as online environments such as multiplayer games and **virtual worlds**, where the emphasis is on authentic communication and interaction. As such, they argue that a connectivist view of learning is more relevant to the types of social technologies that are mainstream today. Connectivism (Siemens, 2005) understands learning and knowledge as something constructed by individuals through their connections with others and also with technology. Technology can act as both a facilitator of personal connections and a repository for one's learning. Technology enables us to access vast amounts of information, and, according to Siemens, informal lifelong learning—through our personal networks, communities of practice, and work-related tasks—are now significant trends in learning. As he puts it, '[k]now-how and know-what is being supplemented with know-where (the understanding of where to find knowledge needed)' (Siemens, 2005, p. 4).

Through our exploration of the development of CALL in this section, we have seen a number of theories of learning reflected in computer-based materials and activities over the years. These theories reflected not only the principal learning beliefs of the time but also developments in hardware and software. However, it is important to realize that what we may think of as 'older' learning theories, such as behaviorism, are still present in technology-based materials available today—in some mobile learning apps, for example. And despite the claims of some edtech companies that their digital tools will automatically enable collaboration, creativity, and independence—all hallmarks of connectivist learning—this is simply not the case. Unless the tool is integrated into a sound pedagogical framework by a teacher who values and promotes collaboration, learner autonomy, and independence, it can just as easily be used for top-down transmission approaches to learning and for controlling students. The interactive whiteboard is a case in point (see Chapter 2).

Corpora and Corpus Linguistics

Another computer-based development that had, and continues to have, profound effects on ELT materials is that of corpus analysis. Corpora—that is, searchable databases of real examples of spoken or written language—have influenced coursebooks, dictionaries, and reference materials, as well as the development of test items for high-stakes language proficiency examinations. The first English-language coursebook with lexical items and a syllabus derived from corpus linguistics, the *Collins COBUILD English Course* (Willis & Willis, 1988), appeared to herald a new dawn in materials writing. As John Sinclair wrote in his foreword to the COBUILD coursebook:

> COBUILD has built up a mass of information from the careful examination of many millions of words, and it offers a new style and balance to the syllabus. [...] Now it is possible, with little trouble, to offer the learner plenty of texts and quite natural English, and this Course opens up experiences in that area.
>
> (Sinclair, 1988, p. i)

COBUILD, and the Lexical Approach it adopted (Lewis, 1993), had limited uptake in ELT, possibly because it was too radical a departure from the traditional grammar-driven syllabus most teachers were familiar with at the time. This was compounded by a lack of access to relevant materials for lower levels and of teacher training (see McEnery & Xiao, 2011, for a discussion of the lack of research studies into corpora-based approaches at secondary school level). However, the influence of corpus linguistics is still evident in many English-language coursebooks today. Coursebook writers often base their choice of lexical items, collocations, and example sentences on American or British English corpora. Learner dictionaries, particularly, have been influenced by corpora, as lexicographers have begun to turn to corpora for examples of real English to illustrate how words are used, rather than relying on artificial-sounding invented sentences to convey meaning.

There are very few empirical research studies into the impact of corpora in primary or secondary school classrooms, in either EFL or ESL contexts. Nevertheless, this is an important area, given its influence on syllabi and coursebooks, and on the development of test items in assessment. A rare piece of research was carried out in a secondary school classroom in Germany with 26 ninth-grade EFL learners aged 13 to 14, using specially designed corpus-based materials and learning activities over a period of four weeks (Braun, 2007). Using a case study approach, the research aimed to investigate the challenges of integrating corpus-based materials and approaches at secondary school level, and also to examine the appropriacy of the chosen corpus for teaching English. A control group worked with traditional coursebook activities, while an experimental group worked with activities based on a corpus of language from video interviews with native English speakers. Findings showed that some—but not all—of the corpus-based activities were perceived by students to be more effective and more useful than traditional computer-based activities; however, post-treatment test scores showed no significant differences in lexical and grammar gains between the two groups. Braun suggests that these secondary students lacked the necessary learner autonomy or inductive and analytical skills to fully interpret corpus data. Overall, she concludes that corpora can provide secondary school language students with positive learning experiences but that some issues remain, such as appropriate task design—how to effectively explore corpora from a pedagogical perspective for secondary-school students.

CD-ROMs

Another example of an early CALL technology which is still with us today is the CD-ROM. Many English-language learner dictionaries, for instance, contain an accompanying CD-ROM that includes audio files of how words are pronounced, as well as a searchable database and/or thesaurus (for example, see the *Oxford Advanced Learner's Dictionary* CD-ROM with the pronunciation of words in American and British English). Recent updates to these tools include being able to access learner dictionaries online or via mobile apps, but the essential functionality of these resources remains the same. CD-ROMs accompanying coursebooks include more multimedia than before, such as high-definition video, but many still include activities from the behavioristic/closed stage of CALL development. See, for example, the *New Headway* iTools CD-ROM series (Soars, Soars, & Davies, 2009), which includes 'older' CALL activities, such as text-reconstruction activities, alongside newer multimedia tools, such as audio and video. One could certainly argue that there is a place for both the old and the new in this type of (usually self-study) CD-ROM. Researchers are in agreement that second language acquisition requires a focus on form and accuracy, and opportunities for more meaning-focused fluency practice, such as listening or reading for comprehension; CD-ROMs these days usually provide opportunities for both. What CD-ROMs are less able to provide are opportunities for students to engage in real communication with other speakers; however, other digital technologies have appeared to fill that gap, as we shall see below.

The Advent of Web 2.0

By the year 2000, digital technologies had undergone a dramatic change. Previously, only those with some knowledge of programming languages such as HTML (Hypertext Mark-up Language) had the skills to create websites, and the internet in its infancy consisted of interlinked but static web pages, visited by those who could afford relatively expensive internet connections. This early internet is now referred to as 'Web 1.0', with websites often created by self-taught amateurs on free hosting services such as Geocities, Angelfire, and Tripod. Dave's ESL Cafe, a website created by Dave Sperling and launched in the mid-1990s, was one of the few available for English language teachers.

By the late 1990s, though, widespread and more affordable internet access and the development of new software allowed for communication, creation, and sharing among a much wider user base. Web 2.0, a term popularized by Tim O'Reilly (2004), had arrived. Now internet users with no specialized programming skills could set up their own personal websites or blogs. The website Blogger was launched in 1999 and allowed users to easily create their own blogs using simple templates. Users could create wikis for their students to use for project work. They could record audio podcasts for their students to listen to out of class—and get their students to do the same for each other. Terms such as 'prosumer'—the user as both 'producer' and 'consumer' of online content—appeared to describe this new phenomenon.

For all the hype, Web 2.0 does have its critics. It has been pointed out that Web 2.0 is simply a development or newer version of Web 1.0, and that they have fundamentally the same underlying technologies. As such, Web 2.0 is not the revolution—in the technical sense—that it is often claimed to be. And although the increase of user content has led to claims of the democratization of the internet, it has also led to the rise of so-called vanity publishing and to a plethora of mediocre, sub-standard, or copied content that is seen by some to be killing creativity (Lanier, 2010). Some critics claim that the internet is rewiring our brains and making us more stupid in the process. For example, Carr (2010) describes how the natural neuroplasticity of the brain appears to be affected by the way we interact with the massive flow of information online: our **working memory** quickly becomes overloaded, affecting the ability of the brain's frontal lobes to concentrate our attention on any one thing. Carr argues that:

> the more we use the Web, the more we train our brain to be distracted
> – to process information very quickly and very efficiently but without
> sustained attention. That helps explain why many of us find it hard
> to concentrate […]. Our brains become adept at forgetting, inept at
> remembering.
>
> (Carr, 2010, p. 194)

Other concerns have been raised about the sustainability of Web 2.0 services, whereby content is externally hosted by **cloud computing** services—that is, software and data are kept on central servers owned by companies rather than on an individual's computer hard drive, and often subject to restricting terms and conditions. For example, if one stores photos or videos on a **social networking site**, such as **Facebook** or **Instagram**, the site's terms and conditions may state that the company then owns that data. Because of this, particular concerns have been raised about privacy and the large amounts of personal data generated on social networking sites that can be used for targeted advertising and possibly other, as yet unclear, commercial services in the future. If wearable technologies such as **smart watches** or **fitness trackers** are recording our weight, exercise, and eating habits, the question of where these data are stored—and who has access to them—becomes important. Insurance companies, for example, might like to base their policy premiums on this kind of information if they were able to access it. Most Web 2.0 services, far from being anarchic collective spaces, are commercial enterprises with their eyes set firmly on monetization (van

Dijck & Nieborg, 2009). For example, the supposedly open collective spaces represented by emblematic Web 2.0 tools such as Blogger and YouTube are, in fact, presently companies owned by Google.

It is important to keep these caveats and criticisms in mind in the face of the relentless hype about the benefits of technology that we are often exposed to. Nevertheless, despite these caveats about Web 2.0, it is clear that access to the internet and the ability to create web-based content has significantly increased. How was this shift from Web 1.0 to Web 2.0 reflected in the ELT classroom? We go on to examine this below.

Online Cultural Exchange Projects

By the mid-1990s, English language teachers who considered themselves 'early adopters' of technology were experimenting with digital tools that supported both **synchronous** and **asynchronous** communication between learners in different contexts. Early examples of language students working online in pairs to practice a **foreign language** took place mainly in college and university contexts, and were known as 'e-tandem exchanges' (O'Dowd, 2014). This term referred to pairs of students with different L1s working together semi-autonomously to learn one another's language, frequently outside of formal classroom instruction—for example, an L1 French speaker learning English interacting with an L1 English speaker learning French. Research into e-tandem exchanges typically focused on the development of linguistic competence, with little, if any, attention being paid to the cultural aspect of these exchanges. However, as the focus of this research broadened, and as teachers in primary and secondary schools began to experiment with online language exchanges, intercultural awareness became a key concern alongside the development of linguistic competence. The growing trend towards investigating intercultural aspects of online communication is reflected in the new terms coined to describe these exchanges, for example 'internet-mediated intercultural foreign language education' (Belz & Thorne, 2006) and 'online (inter)cultural exchange' (O'Dowd, 2007). In primary and secondary schools, some of the earliest online exchanges involved classes of learners in different countries exchanging emails as the basis for culture-based global projects. The terms 'keypals' and 'e-pals', derived from the word 'penpals', were frequently used to describe these projects, which usually took place as part of formal classroom instruction. Initial research into email projects tended to accentuate the positive (O'Dowd, 2014), concluding that such projects not only allowed students to take part in authentic communication in the target language—and to develop their linguistic resources—but also enabled them to undermine cultural stereotyping and to develop intercultural skills and knowledge. Interestingly, this has not always proved to be the case. For example, Kramsch and Thorne (2002) describe an email exchange project between secondary school learners in the USA studying French and learners in France. They found that cultural assumptions were reinforced by different discourse styles, hindering communication. They described a breakdown in communication between these two groups of learners as caused by different 'genres' of communication style, linked to the learners' respective national cultures. However, the view of monolithic 'genres' of culturally linked communication styles has been criticized as over-simplistic (Goodfellow & Lamy, 2009). It has been suggested that, although there may be some cultural differences in online communicative styles, this should be understood as just one of several factors that can hinder communication between two language groups (O'Dowd & Ritter, 2006). For example, wider geopolitical events may negatively affect learners' perceptions of each other; in a 2005 online cultural exchange between students in Spain and the USA, O'Dowd found that the ongoing war in Iraq, and the complex political relationship between Spain and the United States, led many of the Spanish students to react negatively to the idea of an exchange with American students and a focus on American materials during class time (O'Dowd, 2014).

In a similar vein, synchronous, or real-time, text chat programs could be used by learners in different locations to interact with each other. Early research around this form of communication found that learners' oral competence could be indirectly improved by spending time in online text chat rooms (see Payne & Whitney, 2002; Payne & Ross, 2005). Today, video chat software such as **Skype** makes this kind of collaboration between classes even easier, and it is a viable option for primary and secondary schools in many contexts. Large international non-profit organizations such as iEARN, established in 1988, are dedicated to promoting collaborative intercultural cross-curricular projects between classrooms around the world using digital technologies; at the time of writing, iEARN included over 2 million students, 50,000 educators, and 140 participating countries. A similar organization for primary- and secondary-aged students is Kidlink, established in 1990. The extent to which research shows online intercultural exchange projects improving language learning outcomes is something we will discuss in more detail in later chapters.

WebQuests

Real-time communication—whether spoken or written—between learners in different geographical locations was not the only learning opportunity provided by Web 2.0. The ever-growing wealth of information freely available on the internet could also be harnessed for learning opportunities. In 1995, Bernie Dodge coined the term '**WebQuest**' to describe an inquiry-based approach to using the information on the internet. Through guided searches of material on the web, learners are encouraged to transform their findings into a range of products, not just developing essential research skills but also processing the knowledge gained and creating new artifacts, such as posters or presentations. WebQuests became immensely popular with K–12 teachers in many subject areas as well as with EFL teachers around the world, although empirical research studies into their efficacy remained thin on the ground. Indeed, in a review of research into WebQuests, Abbitt and Ophus (2008) concluded that no direct increase in student achievement could be attributed to their use, although a positive impact on learner motivation and improved collaboration skills could be identified.

The extent to which WebQuests were promoted as a particularly effective form of 'technology'-based learning and were taken up enthusiastically by teachers all over the world—especially in North America—is a salutary example of how learning technologies can become popular despite there being very little evidence of their effectiveness. This is a theme we see repeated often and one which continues to this day, whether we are talking about new approaches to teaching and learning, such as 'mobile learning'; software, such as apps; or hardware, such as interactive whiteboards. It is a theme we will return to throughout this volume.

Of course, the history of educational technology does not end with the advent of Web 2.0. More recent hardware developments include interactive whiteboards, mobile devices such as cell phones and tablets, and wearable technology. Developments in software have supported a massive rise in online learning worldwide and particularly in the K–12 sector in North America. These and other more recent developments will be examined in depth in later chapters.

Activity 1.3

Consider your own experience of learning language(s). Have you used any of the digital tools, programs, or approaches that we discussed in this section? If so, how successful do you think they are/were?

Do you have any questions about research into language learning with technology? Note down two or three questions you would like answered. Refer back to your questions regularly while reading this volume to see if you find the answers.

Mapping the Terrain

As we have seen, the concept of learning technologies in language teaching covers a lot of ground: geographically, politically, historically, technologically, theoretically, and, of course, pedagogically. As we saw in Classroom Snapshots 1.1, 1.2, and 1.3 from Japan, Uruguay, and the USA respectively, learning technologies can be used in different ways in different contexts, and the why and how of this is influenced by many factors. This makes our task in this book of reviewing the research into the use of learning technologies in language teaching and learning challenging. And this is why it is especially important that we first map out the terrain—or, in other words, try to describe the learning technologies landscape we will be viewing in very general terms. Although we are limiting our exploration of the research in Chapters 3 and 4 to primary- and secondary-level students, it is a lot more challenging to decide what sorts of contexts and tools to include in our journey. And although we could decide to restrict our exploration only to English language teaching in North America, we would be ignoring one of the key characteristics of new technologies—that is, their ability to travel across borders and the key role that they play in globalization, not just in trade and commerce but also in education. For this reason, although our primary focus will be on research carried out in North American K–12 contexts, we will make regular reference to ESL and EFL contexts from around the world. For example, we will also look at how English is taught in Germany and how other second or foreign languages are taught in various contexts, such as Spanish or French in the USA.

The Digital Divide

To continue with our mapping metaphor, when one talks about technology and geography, one of the first phrases that comes to mind is 'the digital divide'. Typically referring to the difference between resource-rich or 'high-tech' environments and resource-poor or 'low-tech' environments, the term is often used to refer to developed countries, where it is assumed the vast majority of people have access to technology, and developing countries, where the opposite is assumed. Access to computers and related infrastructure is, of course, linked to economic issues such as purchasing power, but the rise of mobile computing has blurred these geographical distinctions somewhat. Low-cost mobile devices have made access to English language provision a reality for millions (for example, via the English in Action project in Bangladesh among others; see Pegrum, 2014). In addition, it has been pointed out that one does not necessarily need access to the latest technology devices in order to carry out effective learning tasks in the language classroom (Yang & Egbert, 2004). Although the digital divide does still exist, we need to avoid simplistic assumptions. The digital divide is present not only in the access—or lack of access—between developed and developing nations; it can also exist within specific countries, for example between urban and rural areas, even within apparently developed nations such as the USA. According to this more nuanced understanding of a digital divide, teachers working in resource-rich countries may find themselves working in resource-poor institutions or classrooms.

The digital divide can also exist within specific classrooms, for example, between learners who have access to technology at home and those who do not. Research has shown that this can significantly affect a learner's ability to carry out homework effectively, for instance, and this can have an impact on grades.

If we look a little more closely at the issue of access and the digital divide in a single context, we see that it can also relate to attitude and/or opportunity. These, in turn, may be linked to socioeconomic and cultural factors. For example, in families where adults use technology for professional or educational purposes, the children are more likely to see digital tools as useful for learning. However, children who grow up in households where the main digital tool may be a gaming console and the primary roles of technology relate to entertainment or shopping are less likely to see digital tools as useful for learning. A UK-based research project entitled *Learning in Families* found that technology played an important role in family learning but that disadvantaged and minority groups reported significantly lower levels of participation in some types of family learning (Grant, 2009). Social support from both peers and family members is key in developing computer competence; this leads Warschauer and Matuchniak

(2010) to suggest that 'many low-income or immigrant youth will have few friends or relatives who are sophisticated users of digital media' (p. 188), highlighting the fact that social factors are more important than technical factors in affecting access to technology.

In addition, we may broaden our definition of a digital divide to include the difference between *effective* and *ineffective* uses of technology for language learning (Yang & Egbert, 2004), regardless of the technology available. And related to this is the divide between those who have the necessary *skills* to use technology effectively and those who do not (Warschauer, 2011). A further digital divide may exist between teachers in terms of *attitude*. For example, when technology is introduced into an institution, some teachers may be willing to learn how to use it effectively while others may be resistant.

Furthermore, a lack of operational proficiency in English may create a digital divide between those who can access and understand materials or websites in English and those who cannot (Walker & White, 2013). Instant machine translation services, whereby text in one language can be easily and instantaneously translated into another, can mitigate this to a certain degree with text, but it is another matter for audio and video content.

Finally, let us not forget that some teachers and learners work in environments where access to the internet or to certain tools, such as social media, may be subject to censorship or surveillance (Pegrum, 2009; Yeok-Hwa Ngeow, 2010).

Criticisms of the Digital Divide

Although the term digital divide has now been in use for several decades, it is not unproblematic. For example, Warschauer (2002) argues that the term is misleading because it suggests a binary distinction between 'haves' and 'have-nots'; in addition, it suggests that simply by giving people hardware, software, and internet access, the digital divide will somehow be overcome. Warschauer, along with other commentators such as Young (2001), argues that simplifying the issue of the digital divide can lead to technological solutionism: the belief that technology can, by itself, fix social problems. Instead, he suggests that technology uses and practices are embedded in specific social contexts and require a range of social and literacy skills; as such, he suggests that the digital divide needs to be reconceptualized as part of a social inclusion agenda.

Payne (2005) provides a helpful overview of the range of critical voices that have been raised against an oversimplification of the digital divide.

He describes how a more nuanced approach examines it from a number of perspectives, including inequalities of social inclusion, gender, and cultural literacy. It is as well to keep this nuanced perspective in mind as we look more closely at the significance of the digital divide in North America.

The Digital Divide in North America

Despite criticisms of the term digital divide, it has proved remarkably tenacious and is used consistently by governments and researchers. Research carried out into the digital divide in Canada and the USA reflects several of the issues highlighted in the previous sections. Furthermore, the research suggests that some of these issues have remained relatively unchanged for at least a decade. Let us first take a look at Canada.

A study carried out by Looker and Thiessen in 2003 examined to what extent rural/urban location, gender, and socioeconomic status affected Canadian high school students' access to and use of digital technologies. They found a digital divide between rural and urban users, between female and male users, and between families with lower versus higher levels of parental education; in each case, the former were less likely to have access to computers in the home. A recent study into the Canadian digital divide (Haight, Quan-Haase, & Corbett, 2014) looked at inequalities in internet access and at more recent phenomena such as the use of social networks. This particular study found that a digital divide in internet access still exists between individuals with lower or higher levels of income and education, between rural and urban communities, between older and younger users, and between immigrants and Canadian-born residents; in each case, the former group has less access. Another report on the digital divide in Canada published by Statistics Canada (Geist, 2013) highlighted the continued difference in access to broadband and wireless internet between higher- and lower-income households across all age groups.

In the USA, similar trends can be identified. Access to digital tools and the internet can be a challenge for low-income communities (Parker, 2008). As in Canada, the level of parental education in the USA can also affect children's internet access. For example, Rideout, Foehr, and Roberts (2010; cited in Warschauer, 2011) found that 91 percent of children whose parents held college degrees had internet access at home, in contrast to 74 percent of children whose parents had not attended college. Data collected by the US Census Bureau in 2014 indicated that just 45 percent of families earning less than $20,000 a year had broadband subscriptions, whereas connection rates for those in higher income brackets—earning $75,000 or more per year—were 91 percent. This recent research indicates a stronger digital divide in the USA within urban communities than between urban and rural communities—67 percent of rural households had broadband internet access versus 75 percent of urban households. The census data also indicated that in disadvantaged urban communities, race and ethnicity correlates with internet access: about a third of African-American and Hispanic households were found to have no broadband connections compared to a fifth of White households and ten percent of Asian households. Warschauer and Matuchniak (2010) found, however, that these differences in access to digital media are narrower between homes with children.

However, some of the discourse surrounding these types of research questions can be problematic. For example, Warschauer (2002) cautions us that African-Americans in the USA are frequently portrayed as being disadvantaged by the digital divide. However, the reality is more complex. Access to the internet for ethnic groups is affected primarily by income—higher-income groups have more internet access, regardless of ethnicity. Perpetuating the stereotype of disconnected minority groups, it is argued, can reinforce social inequalities by implying a social division that is a lot more complex in reality; furthermore, when beliefs in a simplified divide based on these stereotypes inform educational policy decisions, the effects can be marginalizing and patronizing (Jenkins, discussed in Young, 2001, p. 51).

Wider socioeconomic factors affect computer use and internet access not just in the home but also in schools. A comparative study carried out by Warschauer, Knobel, and Stone (2004) into the use of technology in schools within high and low socioeconomic communities found that several factors in lower socioeconomic schools negatively impacted on technology use. For example, these schools tended to have a higher turnover of teaching, administrative, and technology support staff, which made planning for the implementation of technology more difficult. In contrast, the higher socioeconomic schools tended to invest in professional development for staff, had full-time technical support staff, and developed channels of communication between all staff that supported the use of digital networks. Such an environment encouraged teachers to use new technologies with their students; in contrast, schools with little or no support meant that teachers were less confident that equipment would work or that they would receive technical support if necessary. In addition, the lower socioeconomic schools often faced wider challenges, including:

larger numbers of English language learners and at-risk students, larger numbers of students with limited computer experience, and greater pressure to increase test scores and adhere to policy mandates.

(Warschauer, 2011, p. 23)

How does this relate to English language teachers? As we see from the discussion above, access to digital tools and the internet can vary widely at international, national, and state level, and within individual cities or towns, schools, and homes. This would suggest that teachers planning to use technology with their students first need to check not only what technology students have access to but also how gender, cultural literacy, socioeconomic conditions, and parental attitudes may affect the use of digital tools in the home. Teachers cannot simply assume that all their students will be able to carry out **blended learning** activities or homework that requires internet access from home, and this may be the case even in relatively well-resourced schools and environments.

Teachers, Students, and Technology

Like the general public, teachers' attitudes to their students' use of technology can be ambivalent, even when students use technology for school-related or academic purposes. A 2012 online survey of over 2,400 Advanced Placement (AP) and National Writing Project (NWP) teachers in the USA, conducted by the Pew Research Center, found that, overall, the teachers saw the internet and digital technologies as positively influencing their students' writing. These teachers felt that the internet helped their students write more creatively and provided a wider audience for their written work. They felt that the internet encouraged their students to write in a number of different formats or genres, and to write more frequently. These beliefs all reflect a positive view of students' use of technology. However, these same teachers also expressed concerns about the appearance of informal styles of writing in formal written assignments, a concern expressed frequently in society at large. With so much information available online, the teachers were also aware of the importance of teaching their students about plagiarism and fair use. Although 65 percent of the teachers in this survey agreed that the internet enabled students to be more self-sufficient researchers, 83 percent simultaneously felt that the sheer amount of information available online was overwhelming for most students. And although 90 percent of these teachers felt that students' ability to access topics of interest online encouraged and supported their learning, 71 percent felt this same ease of access discouraged students from consulting a wide range of resources during research. These responses reflect a more negative or ambivalent view of students' use of technology and the internet.

Whatever teachers may feel, young people spend a significant amount of time online. In a US-based study, Ito et al. (2009) suggest that outside of school, young people's use of technology is primarily 'friendship-driven' or 'interest-driven'. Friendship-driven online practices are based on socializing, for example, via chatting; sharing music, images, and video on social networking sites and **instant messaging** services; and playing and discussing online games. Those that take part in friendship-driven online activities also display interest-driven behavior online. This also involves communicating, playing games, and media sharing, but reflects a deeper engagement and a creative exploration of technology, for example, by producing complex media themselves. Several large-scale studies have found that this latter creative group is a minority (for example, Kennedy et al., 2009; Salaway & Caruso, 2008). Not all young people, it turns out, are using technology for remixing, self-publishing, or the creation of rich media content. However, the fact that young people spend so much time online and are using digital technologies—and seem to be at ease in doing so—has given rise to the myth of the 'digital native'. This is a concept which we will examine below.

Digital Natives and Immigrants?

Most young people aged eight to 18 spend a significant amount of time online and regularly engage in a range of online activities, although mainly for friendship-driven purposes. This has led many people to believe that children are naturally good at using technology. After all, the argument goes, they have been exposed to digital technologies since birth and have grown up surrounded by technology, so they are naturals when it comes to sophisticated technology use. There seems to be a general consensus that young people are somehow better with technology than older people. To describe this perceived difference, Marc Prensky coined the terms 'digital native' and 'digital immigrant' in 2001, which, at the time, seemed to capture a certain zeitgeist. According to Prensky, digital natives are those who have been brought up with technology and therefore feel comfortable and confident using it; on the other hand, digital immigrants tend to be older, having come to technology later in life. As latecomers to technology, it is argued, they are less comfortable in the online world and, like immigrants learning a new language in a new land, may even have 'accents', such as printing off an email or online article instead of reading it on-screen.

However, the digital native/immigrant distinction has been criticized on a number of counts, not least that of age. One of the fastest-growing groups of internet users are the so-called 'silver surfers', users over the age of 65. In the USA, the number of silver surfers using the internet quadrupled between 2008 and 2010, with 59 percent of seniors using the internet by 2014 and 77 percent owning cell phones (Pew Research Center, 2014a). Nevertheless, according to statistics available at the time of writing, young adults aged 18 to 29 form the biggest demographic of internet users in the USA (97 percent in 2014), followed by teenagers (95 percent), and 30- to 49-year-olds (93 percent) (Pew Research Center, 2014b).

Ultimately, effective use of technology is not determined by age. As we saw in our consideration of the digital divide earlier, access to technology for young people can vary widely due to a range of contextual factors. And, as we see from the AP and NWP teachers' reactions to their students' use of technology discussed above, there are frequently gaps in students' technological know-how. For example, students may not know how to search effectively online and will typically look at only the first two or three search results on a page—which frequently lead to Wikipedia. They may not know how to evaluate the provenance or veracity of information found online. They may be unaware of issues of copyright when reusing images found online. In short, although young people may be comfortable with technology, they are not necessarily adept at using it (Hague & Williamson, 2009) or able to transfer their informal, mainly social, uses of technology into formal learning contexts (Woolfolk, 2012). This has implications for the deployment of learning technologies with primary and secondary learners, as we will see throughout this volume.

Summary

In this chapter, you have been invited to consider your own attitudes to technology in the second/foreign language classroom, and we have looked at some specific classroom contexts in Japan, Uruguay, and the USA which illustrate how context—geographical, economic, political, and pedagogical—can affect the use of learning technologies and attendant outcomes. As we have seen in our discussions so far, the learning technologies terrain is anything but uniform. Indeed, it is very varied. Our consideration of the digital divide, for example, shows us that even within the same city, neighborhood, school, or classroom, learners may have very different options and opportunities for learning with technologies. Learners may also be more or less effective users of technology, regardless of their age. This shows us that it is difficult to generalize when we discuss research within the field of learning technologies. The contextual factors are so many, and the tools so varied, that it is not possible to make sweeping statements such as 'using learning technologies makes students learn English—or any language—better' or 'students learn better with technology'. However, as we will see, some learning technologies can play a positive role in learning outcomes in some contexts, with some learners, depending on how and why they are used. We will explore this in more depth in Chapters 3 and 4. First, though, we will look at general considerations in learning technologies research and examine a number of theories and frameworks that have been proposed by researchers, as well as outline how we are going to review this research in the rest of this book. We turn to all of this in Chapter 2.

2
Learning Technologies: Theories and Frameworks

Preview

In Chapter 1, we identified some of the wider issues that relate to the use of learning technologies in second language teaching. In the first part of this chapter, we will discuss the 21st-century skills and digital literacies that underpin curricula in primary and secondary schools around the world. We also look at how national educational policies frame the implementation of learning technologies in schools across a range of subjects, and what the research has to say about this.

In the area of second and foreign language learning, research in the field of learning technologies is somewhat different from research in other areas, such as grammar or skills. We will explore exactly why and how this is so in the second part of this chapter, where we move on to examine the field of second and foreign language learning technologies research. A number of theoretical perspectives and theories that have informed this research are described, including the interactionist **SLA (Second Language Acquisition)** perspective, sociocultural theories, and ecological perspectives, and we also take a brief look at the range of research methods that have accompanied these various perspectives and theories. We explore a number of conceptual frameworks, and we suggest a way of categorizing the research that will help make sense of the classroom-based studies we review in Chapters 3 and 4.

Twenty-First-Century Skills and Digital Literacies

Child and adolescent learners are not automatically effective users of technology. Key skills such as the ability to evaluate online sources, to filter and manage information, or to synthesize information found online, need to be explicitly taught. For the past few decades, there has been a growing emphasis on the need for schools to help young people acquire these kinds of so-called 21st-century skills. Traditional literacy—reading, writing, and math—is of course still important, but it is argued that to effectively navigate our increasingly digital world, digital literacies—or **multiliteracies** (Cope & Kalantzis, 2000)—are necessary. It is now widely accepted that literacy is a plural concept, hence 'literacies'; in addition, literacies are embedded in social contexts, so are not simply individual skills and competencies but are closely tied to social practices. (For more on the teaching of literacy, see Fu & Matoush, 2015, in this series.)

Within mainstream schooling in the United States, this realization has led to developments such as the National Educational Technology Standards for Students (NETS), which aim to effect curriculum change to support the development of the following broad skills:

1 creativity and innovation
2 communication and collaboration
3 research and information fluency
4 critical thinking, problem solving, and decision-making
5 digital citizenship
6 technology operation and concepts.

(International Society for Technology Education, 2007, no page number)

Many countries have similar initiatives and have seen significant investment in technology in schools, in an attempt to develop learners' digital literacies.

Spotlight Study 2.1

A large-scale comparative study into the state of digital literacies around the world was carried out in 2013 by the International Association for the Evaluation of Educational Achievement (IEA), an independent consortium of national research agencies. Sixty thousand 13- to 14-year-old students (Grade 8) in 3,300 schools in 21 education systems/countries were surveyed, with additional data collected from 25,000 teachers, school principals, and school ICT coordinators working in these schools. The study evaluated students' computer and information literacy, defined as:

an individual's ability to use computers to investigate, create, and communicate, in order to participate effectively at home, at school, in the workplace, and in society.

(Fraillon, Ainley, Schulz, Friedman, & Gebhardt, 2013, p. 17)

It included a focus on the impact of student characteristics and home and school contexts on levels of computer literacy, both within and between countries. A computer-based assessment and questionnaire was delivered to students via USB drives attached to school computers. The assessment required students to carry out a number of practical tasks that required a range of digital skills and led to a larger task, such as creating a webpage with information about a school band competition or collecting and managing information to create a presentation about 'breathing' to present to nine-year-olds. There were a total of four of these larger tasks, and each student completed two, randomly assigned. Results were mapped to a proficiency scale, from level four, the highest, to level one, the lowest. Eighty-one percent of the students surveyed achieved scores that placed them within levels one and three, with the majority at level two. In addition, factors such as students' expected educational attainment, parents' educational level and profession, the number of books in the home, and access to ICT resources at home were all found to positively impact individual test scores across most education systems, although low socioeconomic status cancelled out the positive impact of having access to ICT resources at home. In all but two countries, females scored higher than males on the proficiency scale. Having received ICT instruction in schools also positively affected the test scores in eight countries/education systems (Fraillon et al., 2013). ■

Overall, the implication is clear: young people may appear to be at ease with new technologies, but as Spotlight Study 2.1 shows, there is a range of digital proficiency and in many cases it is fairly low. As educators, we have a responsibility to help learners develop some of the more sophisticated digital skills they lack, and the language classroom is uniquely placed to do so (Dudeney, Hockly, & Pegrum, 2013). We should not expect all of our younger learners to be digitally literate, and conversely, we should not assume our older learners are digitally illiterate.

Digital Literacies Frameworks

Nowadays, we find some element of digital literacies in many national curricula, although terminology may vary. For example, Norway's national curriculum refers to 'digital competency' and Spain's to 'digital competencies', the UK includes 'media literacy' as a key curricular goal, and Australia's national curriculum refers to 'digital media literacy'. In many cases, the understanding is that by focusing on digital literacies in education, we are helping students acquire the skills that they will need for jobs in the future. For instance, a report from the University of Phoenix Research Institute identifies a number of key skills for future workers, which include 'new media literacy' and 'virtual collaboration' among others (Davies, Fidler, & Gorbis, 2011, pp. 6–7).

A number of frameworks for conceptualizing digital literacies have been proposed, and we examine three of these in the following sections. We start with a brief summary of arguably the most theoretical model (Gillen,

2014), which looks at digital literacies from an interdisciplinary perspective and considers its significance in education. Then we describe Walker and White's (2013) framework, which links digital literacies to communicative competence and, as such, ties it to language learning. Finally, we look at Dudeney et al.'s (2013) categorization of digital literacies into four focus areas, a model that suggests specific literacies for each focus. This is perhaps the most practically focused model, and one which provides very specific guidance for teachers wishing to operationalize and assess digital literacies in the language classroom—arguably one of the biggest challenges facing English language educators today.

Digital Literacies as Dialogic Practice

Gillen (2014) proposes a view of digital literacies as emerging dialogic practice. She draws on a number of disciplines, including cultural psychology, education, sociology, and internet linguistics. She adopts a sociocultural ethnographic perspective, suggesting that literacies are socially situated and result from dialogic practices influenced by the wider sociocultural context in which—online and offline—communication takes place. Gillen suggests a theoretical framework for understanding digital literacies that takes into account the idea that knowledge is built through activity, and that meaning-making is achieved within and through digital practices. As such, digital literacy is not a fixed eternal system but rather is constantly in flux because it is 'grounded in people's activities as they participate in diverse kinds of cultural practices' (2014, p. 31).

Key to Gillen's conceptualization is the importance of individual agency, how identity is created and performed online, and how digital environments can provide spaces for ongoing learning. Gillen's research goes beyond the classroom. She analyzes language in a number of communicative environments offered by digital technologies in informal settings, drawing on evidence from research projects. For example, she examines virtual worlds such as **Second Life**, gaming communities, and social networking tools such as Twitter, all spaces for meaning-making and identity creation that exist outside of formal education but are central to many young people's—and adults'—experiences of technologies. Gillen suggests that to operationalize digital literacies in education requires a move towards a more open, flexible, and dialogic pedagogy, in which teachers and students critically engage with a range of digital meaning-making resources. As with many theoretical models, however, Gillen's model remains vague about what teachers should actually do in classrooms with learners.

Digital Literacies as Digital Competence

Another framework for conceptualizing digital literacies—or 'digital competence' as it is called in this case—is proposed by Walker and White (2013). This framework is based on and extends Canale and Swain's (1980) model of **communicative competence** and, as such, links digital literacies to second language acquisition. Like Canale and Swain's model, Walker and White's model of digital competence consists of four elements:

- procedural competence: the ability to effectively use hardware and software
- socio-digital competence: the ability to use technology and language appropriately in a range of online social contexts and knowledge domains
- digital discourse competence: the ability to deploy a range of skills and technical knowledge to produce **digital artifacts**, such as creating and publishing a video, or writing a blog post
- strategic competence: the ability to repair online communications, whether these are affected by technical issues, communication problems, or both.

Walker and White provide examples of what each of these competences means in terms of practical application. For example, at the most basic level, procedural competence means knowing how to turn devices on and off, or how to use basic software programs such as word processors. It also means a wider understanding of how, when, and why to use technology, as well as how to compensate for a lack of technical knowledge and skills. Socio-digital competence might involve knowing how to use different social networking sites appropriately; it includes an understanding of how technology affects language and creates new genres and of what types of language are appropriate to use in different digital contexts. Digital discourse competence brings a range of skills together in creating digital artifacts. Strategic competence allows one to compensate for a lack of ICT skills, for example, by finding alternative solutions to a technical issue; it includes a range of repair skills, such as:

> being able to switch channels, contacting someone by email or social networking if he or she is not answering the phone, rescuing a deleted document, or knowing how to deal with disruptive online interactions such as 'flaming' (heated exchanges in online settings such as email groups or social networks).
>
> (Walker & White, 2013, p. 9)

Four Focus Areas for Digital Literacies

Dudeney et al. (2013) propose a framework for categorizing and operationalizing digital literacies in the ESL and EFL classroom. Based on initial work by Pegrum (2009), they suggest a number of digital skills with four overlapping focus areas: language, information, connection, and (re)design. We will briefly examine each of these in turn.

Language-Based Literacies

Language in the digital age consists of far more than words. An image, a video, a sound, an icon … these are all forms of communication and can often enhance—or even replace—the spoken or written word. Language-based literacies include traditional 'print literacy', but they also include the ability to decode and produce a wide range of online text genres, as follows:

- 'texting literacy': the ability to read and create the abbreviated forms used in text messaging, and to take part in real-time online text chat conversations in socially appropriate ways
- '**hypertext** literacy': the ability to navigate, read, and produce online texts which contain an effective use of **hyperlinking**
- 'multimedia literacy': the ability to interpret and create texts in a range of media, including images, audio, and video
- 'gaming literacy': a macro literacy involving linguistic, multimedia, spatial, and kinesthetic skills in gaming environments
- 'mobile literacy': a key literacy, which Pegrum (2015) suggests is likely to become the principal macro literacy of our time as our digital lives are increasingly mediated via our handheld devices
- 'code literacy': 'the ability to read, write, critique and modify computer code in order to create or tailor software and media channels' (Dudeney, Hockly, & Pegrum, 2013, p. 17).

Information-Based Literacies

These fundamental literacies help us navigate the flood of digital information provided by the internet. They include:

- 'search literacy': the ability to search effectively for information online and to avoid **filter bubbles**
- 'tagging literacy': the ability to label or tag online materials so they are searchable
- 'information literacy': the ability to critically evaluate the provenance and veracity of online information.

Related to this is 'filtering literacy' (knowing how to manage **information overload**), which also includes 'attention literacy' (knowing when to switch off as well as on). Extending this focus on information-based literacies, Pegrum (2015) has more recently highlighted the need for 'data literacy', given the rise of increasingly extensive and complex data generated through our use of a range of connected and smart devices.

Connection-Based Literacies

Our digitally networked world requires that we understand how to nurture and leverage the connections through which we communicate and share information online. Connection-based literacies include:

- 'personal literacy': knowing how to manage your digital identity or online persona
- 'network literacy': the ability to filter information received from your online networks while you, yourself, become a node in these networks by passing on relevant information or news; see also Pegrum (2010)
- 'participatory literacy': the ability to create and produce digital content; this, in turn, includes 'intercultural literacy' when working with others online, for example, as we saw in the online intercultural exchange projects described in Chapter 1.

(Re)design Literacies

The range of digital media available online has encouraged the rise of (re)design literacies, in which original content—typically images, audio, and/or video—is created or changed in order to communicate new meanings. Apart from some technical skills, an understanding of the related issues of copyright and plagiarism is involved in (re)design literacies. The best-known example of a (re)design literacy is 'remix literacy', a macro literacy that includes the ability to recreate and repurpose already-made digital content in innovative ways; examples of this are image memes or YouTube parodies based on news or film clips.

Many national curricula make provisions for the development of digital literacies in schools, and there is general agreement among educators that this is an important area. Nevertheless, it is often challenging for teachers to know how to operationalize these literacies in the classroom. This is particularly true for teachers who may not feel confident with technology themselves or who have received little or no training in how to use technology in a principled manner with learners. Dudeney et al. (2013) suggest a principled and staged approach to integrating these digital literacies into the language classroom, based on an initial needs analysis of students' current levels of knowledge and their perceived needs and wants. This is shown in Figure 2.1.

Increasing complexity		First focus: Language	Second focus: Information	Third focus: Connections	Fourth focus: (Re-)design
	*	Print literacy			
		Texting literacy			
	**	Hypertext literacy	Tagging literacy		
	***		Search literacy	**Personal literacy**	
		Multimedia literacy	Information literacy	Network literacy	
			Filtering literacy	Participatory literacy	
	****	**Gaming literacy**		Intercultural literacy	
		Mobile literacy			
	*****	Code literacy			**Remix literacy**

Figure 2.1 A framework of digital literacies

(Dudeney et al. (2013), Table 2.1, p. 6, reproduced with permission)

The framework in Figure 2.1 provides the organizing principle for a range of activities that can be carried out with adolescent English language learners, permitting them to practice some of these digital literacies. Examples include the following:

- Print literacy: Ask students to analyze and then produce short texts on a single topic for a variety of social media, for example a Twitter tweet, a Facebook status update, or a blog comment. Analyze and discuss the different text conventions, audiences, and effects of their texts.
- Texting literacy: Ask students to decipher and create SMS text messages in English. Encourage them to compare the use of abbreviations and emoticons in English with those of other languages they know.

- Hypertext literacy: Ask students to read short online texts on a single topic with few hyperlinks, a judicious number of hyperlinks, and too many hyperlinks. Discuss the effects of over-hyperlinking and under-hyperlinking on the reader and on authorial voice.
- Multimedia literacy: Encourage students to produce images, audio, and/ or video as part of project work. For example, ask students to each create a video book review by talking to camera about a favorite book. Share the book reviews with the class and/or school.
- Gaming literacy: Encourage students to play educational games in English out of class (see Spotlight Study 4.3).

In their book, Dudeney et al. (2013) provide more examples of language learning activities that help students develop specific digital literacies. These activities attempt to move beyond the realm of theory by providing teachers with ways to work with digital literacies in the classroom, both within the confines of a traditional language syllabus and as a free-standing option. And equally importantly, the authors suggest a number of approaches to assessing digital literacies in the language classroom.

The three digital literacies frameworks described above all emphasize the importance of sociocultural contexts in digital communication, and how digital literacies are tied to the appropriate use of technologies across a range of contexts. They all reflect the notion that digital literacies are not a list of discrete skills that are simply acquired and then checked off. Although digital literacies do include procedural skills—such as how to insert an image into a word-processed document—they also include less clearly defined skills, such as communicating effectively online with others. Bawden (2008) suggests that it is more useful to conceive of digital literacies as a *state* or *condition* that changes over time. As technology evolves and changes, so new skills and literacies emerge and become increasingly important.

Activity 2.1

How digitally literate are you? How digitally literate are your primary or secondary school students? (If you have no access to primary or secondary students, speak to teachers of these age groups). Look at the three digital literacies frameworks described above and choose one against which to measure your and your students' digital literacy. Speak to the students and ask them what technologies they use, how often, what for, etc. See if you can identify their relative strengths and weaknesses with digital literacies. Decide what literacies are most appropriate for which age groups—for primary, for secondary, and for yourself as an adult.

Digital Literacies in Schools

As we have seen, digital literacies appear—at least on paper—in curricula around the world at primary, secondary, and college and university level. We have also seen that, although there is general agreement that schools need to help students acquire 21st-century skills, it is a lot less clear how they should go about doing this. There is a lack of research on the effective integration of digital literacies in school settings (Belshaw, 2011; Hague & Williamson, 2009). There is also a lack of clear guidance for teachers on how best to integrate digital literacies into their classroom practice (Payton & Hague, 2010).

In addition, there are a number of competing discourses surrounding the integration of digital literacies into compulsory schooling curricula (Merchant, 2007). Digital or 'computer' literacy is presented as a set of discrete skills to be acquired, as a tool for learning, and/or as a transformative influence that should affect all aspects of schooling. In the UK, the national curriculum defines digital literacy as a general ability to use computers, and this includes, for example, word processing and database software skills; the sociocultural dimensions of digital literacies that we explored above are frequently ignored. In 2012, the existing ICT curriculum in the UK was withdrawn and replaced by a new Computing Programme of Study, which continues an atomized and discrete skills approach to digital literacies. What is more, the emphasis on providing students with skills needed for the future workplace has been criticized as leading to a business-oriented model of education, involving:

> the co-option of digital, pedagogical practices to support narratives
> of economic growth [...] which subsume educational attainment
> and social justice inside agendas for commodification, marketisation,
> employability and enclosure.

> (Hall, Atkins, & Fraser, 2014, no page number)

The current focus on coding skills within ICT curricula in compulsory schooling—for example, in the UK, Singapore, Israel, and Estonia—and endorsed by senior politicians in the UK and the USA (see Pegrum, 2015) can be seen as one manifestation of this drive towards marketable skills as a key outcome for education. US educator Larry Cuban reminds us of the parallels between the current calls to teach schoolchildren coding skills and earlier drives toward market-focused education:

> Public schools, then, have experienced two spasms of vocationally-
> driven reform. One created the 'old vocational education' in the

early 20th century endorsed by the National Association of Manufacturers and now the 'new vocational education' nearly a century later, endorsed by high-tech CEOs spreading the gospel for teaching children to code and take computer science courses. Then and now, policymakers saw an intimate connection between a strong economy and strong schools.

(Cuban, 2015a, no page number)

Nevertheless, despite criticisms, there is support among educators for teaching even pre-school children the basics of coding, for example via simple iPad apps such as ScratchJr, developed at the Massachusetts Institute of Technology (MIT) with a $1.3 million grant awarded by the National Science Foundation (Ngowi, 2014).

There is also growing support for integrating digital literacies into test-taking. For example, since 2010, the Texas Computer Education Association, in partnership with a digital-curriculum and assessment provider called Learning.com, offers Texas schools a free technology literacy assessment. In 2012–13, almost 137,000 eighth graders in 224 of the state's 1,227 public schools took these assessments, which combine multiple-choice knowledge-based questions with interactive performance-based questions. Research carried out by the providers shows that students generally score well in digital citizenship, a digital literacy defined by ISTE as the ability to 'understand human, cultural, and societal issues related to technology and practice legal and ethical behavior' (International Society for Technology Education, 2007). Students also score well in technology operations and concepts, but less well in online research and information fluency, critical thinking, and problem-solving (Flanigan, 2014).

Another example comes from Connecticut, where two state-led consortia—the Partnership for Assessment of Readiness for College and Careers and the Smarter Balanced Assessment Consortium—developed online assessments tied to the Common Core State Standards (CCSS) for use from 2015. Completing these assessments successfully requires the deployment of specific digital literacy skills.

Technology and Educational Policy

As we have seen above, many countries—and states—have educational policies aimed specifically at the teaching of ICT skills or digital literacies in mainstream schooling. However, it is not just these more overt policies that affect how technology is used in schools. Large-scale educational reforms can also impact on the investment, deployment, and even effectiveness of technology in schools and classrooms. Let us take a brief look at two examples: the introduction of the Common Core State Standards in the USA and the introduction of interactive whiteboards in the UK.

The Common Core State Standards (CCSS)

The precursor of the CCSS, the bipartisan No Child Left Behind Act (NCLB) was adopted in 2001 with the goal of ensuring basic proficiency for all students in the key areas of reading and math by 2014. This set the educational agenda in the USA for the coming years: under NCLB, schools, districts, and states were evaluated on the percentage of students passing standardized tests in reading and math. However, when it became increasingly clear that the goal of NCLB was not being met, with many schools not achieving the necessary scores, the CCSS were proposed as a means of more tightly defining what children are expected to know at each grade level across the USA. Up to this point, the 50 individual US states—with a total of 14,000 school districts—had set their own standards and approaches, making comparisons in educational achievement between states difficult. The CCSS were adopted by 45 states in 2010, encouraged by the access to federal funding that this entailed. The CCSS are not a series of curricula; rather, they describe in general terms the skills that children in each grade should acquire. The CCSS and the ways they have been interpreted across the USA have led to heated debate. A detailed review of controversies surrounding the CCSS is beyond the scope of this volume, but see, for example, Liebtag (2013) for an overview.

Whether or not one agrees with the CCSS, one undeniable effect has been a move—started under NCLB—towards ever more standardized tests, which are increasingly taking the form of online assessments, both **formative** and **summative**. Some of these online assessments are developed specifically for ELLs and some for students with special educational needs. For example, federal grants totaling $16.8 million were awarded in 2011 and 2012 to two consortia of states—the Assessment Services Supporting ELs through Technology Systems (ASSETS) and the English Language Proficiency Assessment for the 21st Century (ELPA21) Consortium—to design and develop online assessment of English language proficiency. Both consortia aim to have their tests operational between 2015 and 2016. It has been argued that standardized high-stakes testing can unfairly penalize ELLs because of additional linguistic challenges and culturally biased topics. (For a detailed discussion of second language testing in the context of NCLB, see Jang, 2014, in this series.)

Research supports the notion that the standardized testing required by NCLB and the CCSS has affected how technology is used in schools. Preparation for tests means that teachers and students often use tutorial or 'drill and kill' software programs rather than project-based, more creative uses of technology (Warschauer, 2011). In a national survey in the USA, for example, 50 percent of all teachers stated that they sometimes or often used drill and practice programs in their teaching, and 69 percent stated that their students sometimes or often use computers to learn or practice basic skills (Gray, Thomas, & Lewis, 2010). Given the emphasis placed on these kinds of activities by teachers and students, motivated in large part by standardized testing, one would expect the research to provide evidence of their effectiveness. Unfortunately, this is not the case, as we will see in Spotlight Study 2.2.

Spotlight Study 2.2

A software program called the Waterford Early Reading Program was rolled out to Los Angeles Unified School District kindergarten and first-grade students in an attempt to better support the development of their literacy skills. The estimated total cost to buy and then sustain the program was estimated at $64 million. The software focused on developing basic literacy skills, including letter and word recognition, phonological awareness and letter sounds, and reading comprehension. The district's print reading text and curriculum, called Open Court, covered the same principles. The software option was seen as a way of providing additional study time for students in low-achieving schools to develop their reading skills, in an engaging format and in a mode that could be more easily adapted to their individual level. A two-year evaluation compared classes using the Waterford program with classes not using it and found no benefits from its use. It was found that the students used the software instead of—not in addition to—classroom-based literacy instruction, so they had no additional literacy practice. ELLs in particular found the software confusing and uninteresting, and the lower their proficiency, the more disengaged they were, both with the software and with the print versions of Open Court. In other words, the students who benefited the least were those who were supposed to benefit the most from the program.

(Llosa & Slayton, 2009; described in Warschauer, 2011)

Spotlight Study 2.2 is not the only research that casts doubt on the effectiveness of tutorial CALL or drill-based software. Wenglinsky (2005) carried out an analysis of test score data from the large US National Assessment of Educational Progress (NAEP) and found that using computers for drills and practice in math and in language arts—for grammar and punctuation—had *negative* correlations with student scores. On the other hand, positive correlations were found with more creative uses of computers. As Warschauer summarizes:

> if we wish to increase academic achievement, students should principally use the computer as *a tool to think with* – to carry out research, collect and analyze data, explore ideas through games and simulations, and write authentic texts – rather than as a tutor.

(Warschauer, 2011, p. 10)

In addition, when considering the move towards widespread standardized online testing created by the CCSS, it is as well to recall the economic and political interests involved. Providing online standardized formative and summative tests—and content to prepare for these tests in the form of software packages—is very big business, and educational publishers are well aware of this. Commercial and educational interests do not always coincide, and there are educators who caution us against an unquestioning move towards standardized testing and the mass adoption of software packages and devices through which to deliver it (for example, Selwyn, 2014). Certainly, it behooves us to be aware of the commercial and economic interests accompanying education reforms that work closely with the multimillion-dollar educational technology and publishing industries (Watters, 2014). The rise of the interactive whiteboard is another salutary example of this.

Interactive Whiteboards

Interactive whiteboards, or IWBs, first appeared in significant numbers in UK classrooms in the early 2000s. The UK government allocated up to £10 million between 2003 and 2004 for the introduction of IWBs into primary schools as part of its National Literacy Strategy and National Numeracy Strategy. This decision was, in great part, a response to the political climate of the time: the development of ICT skills in schools was seen as fundamental if Britain was to remain competitive in an increasingly globalized world. It was felt that innovative technologies such as IWBs would support better learning in a whole-class setting; indeed, the dominant discourse of the time claimed that IWBs would 'transform' and 'revolutionize' teaching and learning (Twiner, 2010, p. 38). This resulted in the top-down implementation of educational hardware in schools, driven by the technology itself rather than by any underlying pedagogical principles or research studies. It was a strategy to be replicated in countries around the world—at least in those that had the resources to spend on costly IWBs. According to Thomas and Cutrim Schmid:

[t]he integration of interactive whiteboards in classrooms around the world over the last decade provides a fascinating case study of the current state of pedagogy and increasingly interventionist role adopted by governments in directing education policies and national curricula.

(Thomas and Cutrim Schmid, 2010, p. xx)

Integration of IWBs in classrooms also provides a fascinating case study of technological determinism, in which technology itself is seen as somehow inherently capable of ensuring effective pedagogy and enhanced student attainment. As has happened with much education technology in the past (Selwyn, 2011), IWBs were initially touted as harbingers of a new dawn of learning. However, as Laurillard (2008, p. 1) reminds us, 'education is on the brink of being transformed through learning technologies; however, it has been on the brink for some decades now.'

The fact is that research into the effectiveness of IWBs reveals that the technology does not live up to the hype. Factors such as the way teachers use the IWB, the amount of professional development they have received, the materials used, the classroom context, and students' motivation, expectations, and attitudes will all have a bearing on the relationship between the IWB and student attainment. It is therefore very difficult to prove that IWBs have any direct impact on learning in any discipline. Research findings have pointed to the importance of professional development and training in IWB use for teachers, as well as how staff consultation on the implementation of IWBs can lead to greater acceptance and use (Miller & Glover, 2010).

The appearance of IWBs in EFL contexts can also be dated back to the early 2000s, with boards appearing in British Council teaching centers in many countries around the world. As in mainstream schooling in the UK, it tended to follow a top-down implementation model, a policy that was soon taken up by other language teaching schools in the private EFL sector (Dudeney & Hockly, 2012). The introduction of IWBs into English language classrooms frequently responded to a perceived need—usually by language school managers and directors—to keep up to date and to be seen as having the latest equipment. Coupled with pressure from IWB manufacturers working with ELT publishers, IWBs were promoted as the latest must-have teaching device (Hockly, 2013a). Rarely was the introduction of IWBs into the classroom solicited by teachers or students. Even less frequently was reference made to the improvements in student learning that might be expected to follow, as this research was simply not available. What are available and well documented are the pros and cons of using IWBs in the classroom (see Moss & Jewitt, 2010, for a detailed description of these, with references to specific research studies). High on the list of advantages are increased engagement and motivation for learners, while high on the list of disadvantages are technical challenges, the significant cost of many IWBs, and a general lack of support and training for teachers when they start using this technology. Some of the pros and cons of the use of IWBs are illustrated in Classroom Snapshot 2.1.

Classroom Snapshot 2.1

A group of twelve eight-year-old students are studying the national curriculum in an 'immersion' primary school in Spain, where classes are taught in English. Four of the students are native speakers of English, while the other eight have Spanish as their first language. The IWB is used in almost all lessons, primarily by the teacher standing at the front of the class. Typical content shown on the IWB includes games linked to the curriculum, for example multiplication games to practice multiplication tables; pictures to illustrate new words or concepts; and audio and video content, for example films. For most of the children, this is their first experience with IWBs and they have been using them for less than a year.

The children take part in semi-structured interviews with a researcher-teacher about their views on the use of the IWB in their lessons. Here is a selection of their comments:

- 'I like the multiplication games because I can learn the times tables very easily … if we did not have the IWB it would be boring and harder to learn.'
- 'We see the images and when we don't understand it helps us a lot.'
- 'Sometimes when she [the teacher] speaks very fast, we focus on the pictures on the IWB. We see the big and colorful images and they stick in our minds. It's easier to understand them.'
- 'It's very helpful because you don't have to go to the computer and touch it; you can do it with your hand.'
- 'The teacher uses it most of the time.'
- 'Every time we play a film it freezes.'
- 'The teacher does not know how to manage the IWB sometimes.'

(Yáñez & Coyle, 2010, pp. 446–57) ∎

As we see from these children's comments on their experiences of the IWB, they identify certain elements very positively, such as the games and multimodal, multimedia content that IWBs support very well. In the first three comments, the children identify this as motivating and helpful for their comprehension. The tactile nature of the IWB is another positive element. However, as a fixed board at the front of the room, IWBs tend to be monopolized by the teacher, encouraging a teacher-centered transmission or 'presentational' approach to learning (Reedy, 2008); this is reflected in the fifth comment. The students' desire to be allowed to touch and use the board more often themselves was an important overall finding in this and other studies (for example, Solvie, 2004; Hall & Higgins, 2005). Another significant disadvantage, also well documented in the research, are the technical challenges that teachers can face in using IWBs (for example, Hall & Higgins, 2005; Shenton & Pagett, 2007; Wood & Ashfield, 2008).

Despite the lack of research evidence that IWBs are directly responsible for improved learning outcomes, they are a fact of life in many ELT classrooms today. The initial debate between IWB skeptics (for example, Dudeney, 2006) and IWB evangelists, notably publishers and IWB manufacturers, has given way to a more measured response in which exploration of the specific affordances of IWBs is seen as the way forward. For example, the European-Union-funded research project Interactive Technologies in Language Teaching found that the lack of appropriate IWB materials and effective teacher training are major challenges to the integration of IWBs. This particular EU project seeks to redress this situation by providing free online resources, such as a teaching handbook and a video bank of teachers using IWBs, to illustrate best practices.

CCSS and IWBs: The Implications

CCSS and IWBs appear to be very different. The CCSS are the outcome of a national educational *policy*, whereas IWBs are examples of *hardware* implemented on a national scale, as part of a national educational policy. Nevertheless, both examples clearly reflect how top-down educational reform policies can intersect with educational technology and drive the educational agenda in directions that educators may find contentious. Neither the CCSS emphasis on standardized—increasingly online—testing and the concomitant use of drill-based software packages nor the worldwide initiative with IWBs has a solid grounding in research showing improved learning outcomes. As such, they provide a cautionary tale. Technology is not a magic bullet.

Activity 2.2

Can you identify a national technology-related educational policy that has made an impact on the context in which you teach? Is your example similar to the CCSS policy described above—a set of *educational guidelines, strategies*, or *policies* imposed by a government or education ministry? Or is it similar to the IWB example—a *hardware-driven policy*, introduced at school, state, or national level? Or is it similar to Spotlight Study 2.2—which describes a *software-driven policy* like the Waterford Early Reading Program? What issues have arisen for teachers and students as a result of this policy?

As we have seen, one of the biggest criticisms of large-scale adoption of policies, hardware, or software is that it is often done with no supporting research. As Cuban points out, the NCLB Act includes the phrase 'scientifically based research' 110 times, but many policies reflect political realities rather than the findings of rigorous research:

> [T]he historical record is rich in evidence that research and evaluation findings have played a subordinate role in making educational policy. Often, policy choices were (and are) political decisions.
>
> (Cuban, 2015b, no page number)

Policies can be implemented at a national level, but they can also be developed and implemented at state or even district levels.

We now turn from the politics and policies of learning technologies to the research. Despite the paucity of research in many government-led policy decisions, we will see that learning technologies research does indeed have a rich tradition in the field of English language teaching and learning.

CALL Research

In the following sections, we use the term 'CALL', rather than 'learning technologies', precisely because of this rich research tradition in which it is the most commonly used term. It is worth noting, however, that in the K–12 sector in North America, it is more common to refer to 'literacies' research, particularly within the framework of digital literacies, multiliteracies, and 21st-century skills (Ware & Hellmich, 2014). Nevertheless, since the term 'CALL research' is still very widely used, including in studies that focus on ELLs and learning technologies, we use it in this chapter.

We now have around 30 years of CALL research to draw on. The field has grown rapidly, with a proliferation of research studies and specialized journals in which to publish this research. CALL research draws on a number of disciplines, including second language acquisition theory, **psycholinguistics**, **human–computer interaction**, and **natural language processing**, among others. Not surprisingly, therefore, it has suffered from a lack of a single unifying theoretical framework against which to evaluate its efficacy. This can lead to a rich body of informed work; however, it can also lead to a confusing array of anecdotal case studies that do little to contribute to a sound research base (Egbert & Petrie, 2005; Levy, 2016).

The debate over how to focus research in CALL studies also goes back several decades (Oxford, 1995; Holland, Kaplan, & Sams, 1995). For example, Chapelle's (1997) seminal article 'CALL in the Year 2000: Still in Search of Research Paradigms?' argued for an SLA research agenda with:

> a perspective on CALL which provides appropriate empirical research methods for investigating the critical questions about how CALL can be used to improve instructed SLA.

> (Chapelle, 1997, p. 21)

Chapelle proposed an interactionist SLA perspective, which is explored below. CALL researchers have also used a sociocultural perspective, a **systemic functional linguistics** perspective, an intercultural perspective, a situated learning perspective, a **design-based research** perspective, an **ecological perspective**, and so on. Each perspective has its own primary focus or agenda—and its blind spots. Whatever perspective underpins a research study, the researcher needs to make it salient for the reader and to be aware of what that focus might leave uncovered (Egbert & Petrie, 2005). And, of course, there is also research—often practitioner-based **action research** projects—with no explicit theoretical basis at all; Hubbard (2009) refers to this as *atheoretical* CALL. Thus, there are differences in the role of theory in formal research studies and in classroom teaching. In a more formal research situation, a specific theory—or theories—may be chosen, and hypotheses formed and then tested against qualitative and quantitative data. In the classroom, however, a teacher may be experimenting with a new approach and new technologies, and a theory, framework, or model may be created or arise from the data.

As we saw in Chapter 1, technology in language learning has developed over the years, and the seemingly fragmentary research in the field is arguably best pulled together in volumes such as those edited by Egbert and Petrie (2005); Levy and Stockwell (2006); Stockwell (2012); Thomas, Reinders, and Warschauer (2013); and Farr and Murray (2016). As Levy points out:

[g]iven such variables as the number of technologies in use, the variety of potential settings, the rate of change at which technology is evolving, grasping a sense of the whole is challenging and difficult to embrace.

(Levy, 2016, p. 103)

Reading these volumes will give the interested reader a rich understanding of the most important CALL research perspectives and their development.

One way to navigate through the many perspectives and theories in CALL studies is to orient oneself with the help of a framework, such as that suggested by Hubbard and Levy (2016) and developed from Hubbard's earlier (2009) work. We will explore their framework briefly in Activity 2.3.

Activity 2.3

The table below summarizes Hubbard and Levy's framework, which categorizes the theoretical presence in CALL research studies into seven broad areas. A definition for each of these terms is provided on the right. Can you insert the three missing terms—'theory adaptation', 'theory borrowing', and 'theory construction'—in the correct places?

1 _____	A theory from another domain (e.g. psychology) is applied unchanged to a CALL study.
2 **theory instantiation**	A broad learning theory (e.g. activity theory) is applied to the technology under study, and both are explicitly analyzed.
3 _____	A theory from another domain (e.g. psychology) is applied to a CALL study, but it then needs to be changed due to the research findings.
4 **theory ensemble**	Several theories are applied to a single CALL study so as to allow for multiple perspectives.
5 **theory synthesis**	Several theories are applied to a single CALL study, and from the insights derived, a new theoretical entity (e.g. theory, framework, or model) emerges.
6 _____	A new theory, specifically related to CALL, is produced. It may be informed by previous theories, but is independent enough to be considered a native CALL theory.
7 **theory refinement**	Over time, theories are developed and improved, or conversely, fail or are dropped, as more data from various studies emerge.

As you read the research summaries, Spotlight Studies, and Classroom Snapshots in this and later chapters, consider which of Hubbard and Levy's categories helps to place or explain each one. We start with an example of theory construction via a practitioner-based research project in Classroom Snapshot 2.2.

Classroom Snapshot 2.2

A group of 12 intermediate learners, aged about 16 to 25, are attending an EFL class as part of an intensive summer study program in the UK. Learners are working in pairs and each learner is holding their own mobile device; in some cases this is an Android, iPhone, or Blackberry smart phone, and in some cases it is an iPad. On the board is a list of ten photos that the learners need to find and share: a photo of a pet, a good friend, a celebration, a view, a selfie, a child or parent … The learners show each other one photo from each category on their device screens and ask each other questions to find out more about each photo. The teacher moves around the class and monitors the pairs, noting down language errors for later group correction. The teacher stops the activity when the first pair seems to have finished. She then conducts feedback by asking each student to share one or two interesting things they found out about their partner. The activity ends with a review of the errors that the teacher collected in the monitoring stage. The aim of the activity is for the learners to get to know each other through a personalized ice-breaker oral interaction activity using their own devices, and for the teacher to get an idea of the levels of speaking proficiency within the group.

(Hockly, 2013b) ■

The activity described in Classroom Snapshot 2.2 is from a classroom-based action research project carried out by Hockly (2013b). The study took place over a two-week period with two groups of international EFL students, aged mainly 16 to 25, in a private language school in the UK. Taking as its starting point Laurillard's (2012) assertion that classroom practitioners need to become designers of effective learning experiences, the study trialed a BYOD (bring your own device) approach with two different classes: a class of beginner/low elementary students and a class of intermediate students. Learners brought their own mobile devices to class—smartphones and tablets in this context—and used these to complete certain language tasks designed by the teacher on an evolving basis. The aim of the project was to explore the choices and challenges involved in designing communicative mobile-device-based classroom tasks within the confines of an imposed syllabus, defined by the use of a coursebook.

Through the experience of working with these two groups of learners, six parameters for the effective design and sequencing of mobile-based communicative tasks emerged. First, the hardware, or devices, and internet access that students have, both in and out of class, affect the design of tasks that require connectivity. For example, sharing photos taken for homework out of class time requires students to have internet access. Second, the mobility of devices, students, and/or the learning task itself needs to be taken into consideration. A third consideration is the technological complexity of tasks, which needs to be balanced with a fourth consideration, the demands on students' linguistic and communicative competence. As a rule of thumb, it is not a good idea to set tasks that are both technically *and* linguistically challenging because less proficient students can feel overwhelmed. Fifth, the learning theory underpinning the task—whether behaviorist or communicative—needs to be taken into account as it affects the language that students need to produce. Finally, the effects of the educational/learning context on students' attitudes and motivation towards learning with mobile devices can support—or undermine—efforts to work with devices in and out of class.

Theoretical Perspectives in CALL Research

We now turn to some of the theories, or perspectives, indicated in Hubbard and Levy's framework from Activity 2.3. These theories have formed the basis of a significant amount of CALL research to date. Unsurprisingly, CALL research has been influenced by second language learning theories (see Mitchell, Myles, & Marsden, 2013, for a detailed consideration of mainstream SLA theories). It has also been influenced by academic disciplines such as sociolinguistics, psycholinguistics, and computational linguistics; by developments in technology hardware, from CD-ROMs to mobile devices; and by developments in software, for example virtual worlds, computer games, and social networking sites. In this section, we will take a brief look at some of the theoretical perspectives that underpin a significant amount of formal CALL research.

The Interactionist SLA Perspective

The interactionist perspective suggests that communication—that is, interaction—between speakers is a key component of language acquisition, and that interlocutors will typically modify their language to ensure that they are mutually intelligible (for more on the interactionist perspective specifically with regard to learning in the primary and secondary school classroom, see Oliver & Philp, 2015, in this series). As we saw above, Chapelle's (1997) seminal article argued for a CALL research agenda based on SLA interactionist research. According to Chapelle, the two most important research questions to be addressed are 'What kind of language does the learner engage in during a CALL activity?' and 'How good is the language experience in CALL for L2 learning?' (Chapelle, 1997, p. 22).

As one of the first to articulate a coherent CALL research agenda, Chapelle has been particularly influential in shaping the SLA research perspective. Despite criticisms that this represents too narrow a perspective (for example, Salaberry, 1999), Chapelle (1999) argued that inquiry in the fields of educational technology, computers and collaborative learning, artificial intelligence, computational linguistics, and corpus linguistics all boil down to one essential question for CALL: how to promote the development of L2 communicative competence for the language learner. Acknowledging that the interactionist approach does have a narrow linguistic focus, she points out that it can still be productive for the design of certain research questions and tasks (Chapelle, 2005).

Sociocultural Theory

Proponents of a sociocultural perspective in CALL research emphasize that technology use takes place within specific sociocultural contexts and cannot be divorced from these. Drawing on the work of Vygotsky, sociocultural theory revolves around the idea of **mediation** and how tools—such as computers or even language—transform human activity. A key concept in sociocultural theory is that of social learning, whereby children—and, by analogy, language learners—are encouraged to gradually develop their competence through interaction with more knowledgeable others, who scaffold and support their learning in the **Zone of Proximal Development (ZPD)**. Language learners need to interact with others in the target language—for example, with other students and the teacher— in meaningful contexts, and they need to pay attention to the form and meaning of new language in order to acquire it. Another concept in sociocultural theory is that of developmental processes and histories—the idea that we can only understand certain mental functioning and behaviors if we put them in their sociohistorical and cultural contexts. (For more on sociocultural theory and learning in the primary and secondary school classroom, see de Oliveira & Schleppegrell, 2015; Fu & Matoush, 2015, in this series.)

Mark Warschauer is arguably one of the best-known CALL researchers working from a sociocultural theory perspective. He describes this as being mainly concerned with the study of technology related to issues of culture, literacy, and identity. According to Warschauer, sociocultural CALL research has taken place primarily in three contexts:

(1) technology-enhanced learning in individual language classes,
(2) language learners' informal uses of new technologies outside the classroom, and (3) telecollaborative exchanges between classes.

(Warschauer, 2005, p. 43)

Some examples of CALL research underpinned by a sociocultural research agenda can be found in Chapter 1 (see, for example, the discussion of Kramsch & Thorne, 2002, and O'Dowd, 2014, on page 22). In another email exchange study between French and American students, Thorne (2003) found that the tool itself—email in this case—took on different meanings for the participants. For example, the American students came from more privileged backgrounds and had much more experience than the French students of using technology for communication; they preferred instant messaging for informal communication and found email to be formal and restrictive. The American participants therefore felt that the use of email for this cross-cultural exchange was inauthentic, and the project carried less value for them because of this. This particular project clearly highlights how the appropriacy of a particular technology—or the 'medium'—is influenced by local cultural and/or historical factors, which then shape the user's perspective.

From this example, we can see that a sociocultural perspective can bring unexpected insights to CALL research, insights which can be overlooked by a purely interactionist SLA research approach. An interactionist SLA approach might focus primarily on the language produced by the learners in such an intercultural email exchange and examine learners' use of repair strategies, for example, with less attention paid to the wider context. It is not that the sociocultural perspective should replace the SLA perspective but simply that they have very different research agendas and may be seen as providing complementary information. Thorne's (2003) study highlights the difficulty in drawing comparisons between CALL research studies, when their research questions and approaches can be so different.

The Ecological Perspective

The ecological approach to SLA research is associated with the work of Kramsch (2002) and particularly van Lier (2004a), who wrote an influential volume called *The Ecology and Semiotics of Language Learning: A Sociocultural Perspective*. The ecological approach has much in common with sociocultural/sociohistorical perspectives, having as its primary focus how learners interact with the wider environment, including beyond the classroom. The ecological perspective implies a holistic approach to understanding language acquisition and, as such:

> language is not studied as an isolated, self-contained system but rather in its natural surroundings, i.e. in relation to the personal, situational, cultural, and societal factors that collectively shape the production and evolution of language.
>
> (Kramsch & Steffensen, 2008, p. 18)

How is the ecological perspective relevant to the role of technology in language learning? Developments in technology have provided learners with the means to take their language learning far beyond the classroom walls, where a wide range of 'personal, situational, cultural, and societal factors' (Kramsch & Steffensen, 2008, p. 18) come to the forefront. The internet, and mobile devices in particular, provide many opportunities for what Thorne (2009; 2010) calls language learning 'in the wild'. Individuals increasingly have the opportunity to develop their identities as English learners in non-academic social contexts, on their own terms and from a relatively young age. For example, Cilesiz (2009) describes a group of Turkish teenagers exploring and developing their identities as English language learners—and future professionals—online in internet cafés. Spotlight Study 4.3 shows teenagers in Sweden developing their English language abilities as members of an online gaming community. Technology is becoming increasingly ubiquitous and is used for communication across multiple contexts. As Thorne and Black point out:

> for many individuals, performing competent identities in second and additional language(s) now involves internet mediation as or more often than face-to-face and nondigital forms of communication.
>
> (Thorne & Black, 2007, p. 149)

Readers interested in exploring the development of ecological approaches to SLA are encouraged to read Kramsch and Steffensen's (2008) overview of this approach; for our own purposes, suffice it to say that an ecological approach in learning technologies research is arguably the broadest. It takes into account dimensions explored in sociocultural approaches, including notions of self and identity (see van Lier, 2004a, 2004b). It also views learning through a wider economic, political, technological, and even philosophical lens, taking into account the very specific temporal and spatial contexts in which interactions take place.

The Unique Features of CALL Research

As we have seen from the discussion in this chapter, the CALL research panorama is wide and studies are motivated by a multiplicity of theories, viewpoints, and perspectives. On the one hand, we have support for multiple approaches, such as those included in CALL research volumes; on the other hand, we have theorists who are less enamored of this so-called theoretical pluralism (for example, see Gregg, 1993). What is certain is that CALL research does have a number of unique features. Levy (2016) reminds us that these features include the wide range of settings where research can take place, for example school, university, at home, or virtually. Research may be carried out both inside and outside the classroom, in formal and informal technological settings, and in resource-rich and resource-poor contexts. Research can include personal technologies or institutional technologies. Participants in research need a range of digital literacies. Research can be based on theory or emerge from practice. Finally, a wide range of theories and frameworks can be drawn on to support and develop CALL research. Indeed, we have seen many of these features in the Classroom Snapshots and Spotlight Studies included so far in this volume.

Research Methods and Learning Technologies

With the advent of Web 2.0 and especially the rise of social media, there has been an increase in opportunities for second language learning in both formal and informal contexts. In the age of behaviorist or tutorial CALL, research tended to focus on experimental contexts, with control groups and directly measurable outcomes. Much of this early research took place with university-age language learners. There are a number of possible reasons for this: researchers themselves were often working at universities, access to still-expensive computers and networks was mainly available in higher education institutions, and early tutorial CALL materials were aimed mainly at adult learners. As opportunities for language learning aided by technology have expanded—often well beyond the classroom walls—a greater range of research methods has come into play, with a wider range of age groups.

Reviewing some of the research in the current age of social media, Meskill and Quah (2013) identify three main foci in contemporary CALL studies: firstly, those that focus mainly on the online learning environment and its affordances; secondly, those that focus on socioaffective aspects; and thirdly, those that focus on pedagogical processes and effects, such as online task design, teacher interventions and behaviors, learner training—for example, for peer review of online work—and learners' perceptions of their online learning experiences. Through the description of a number of research studies—mainly carried out with adult learners and frequently in university and college contexts—Meskill and Quah show how a range of methods of inquiry are being deployed in the field of CALL research. As they point out, 'New uses of new technologies inspire new inquiry. [...] Like internet practices generally, research design is always evolving.' (2013, p. 52). Methods of data collection in these studies include focus groups and interviews with students and teachers, examination of learner output, video recordings, digital records and transcripts of online interactions, questionnaires, and learner self-reports and perceptions of learning events, as well as the tracking of instructional practices, tasks, and teacher language and its impact.

There is no single research method that is better than any other. The method chosen will depend on the area under investigation, the technology used, and the aim of the researcher; indeed, the outcomes of research should depend on the questions asked, whatever the field of inquiry. More experimental treatments, such as those linked to early CALL, are still appropriate to some research agendas. For example, if researchers want to measure the effect of using a specific vocabulary learning mobile app, they might want to use an experimental approach, with one experimental group and one control, or comparison, group of language learners in the same school. Such a study would use pre- and post-treatment test scores of both groups as a measurement of effectiveness. Indeed, some research into the effectiveness of learning vocabulary via **SMS** text message has used just this approach. For example, a 16-week-long study was undertaken with 28 Iranian university students studying academic English. The students received ten words and example sentences twice a week via SMS, and were exposed to a total of 320 new words. A control group studied the same vocabulary using a dictionary. Post-test scores showed an improvement for all students, with no significant difference between the two groups. However, a delayed post-test showed significantly better retention of the vocabulary by the SMS group (Alemi, Sarab, & Lari, 2012).

Clearly, an experimental approach would be less appropriate for a study into language learning in informal contexts outside of the classroom, such as via an online social networking site or in online games. In these contexts, it is nearly impossible to isolate a single factor that can explain learning outcomes. Here an ethnographic approach makes more sense, where the researcher becomes part of the community, observing and recording detailed data over a period of time. According to Harrison and Thomas:

> [r]esearchers following this approach must learn the language or discourse of communication, identify the key concepts associated with the shared social interaction taking place between individuals and groups, and decode this shared knowledge and cognition from the viewpoint of an observer who has gained deep insights into the community.
>
> (Harrison & Thomas, 2009, p. 115)

For example, Gillen (2014) adopts a sociocultural, ethnographic perspective based on activity theory in observing how two teenage boys engage in an online game in English, their L2. She documents how they draw on a wide range of cognitive, linguistic, and communication strategies, which emerge through their active participation in the game. This approach fits well with a social constructivist theory of language learning (see Chapter 1), in which individual learning is understood to be part of an emergent social and collaborative process that takes place within a wider cultural context.

Making Sense of the Research

Given the wide range of CALL research perspectives, frameworks, and methodologies on offer, it is a significant challenge to categorize studies in a meaningful way. We saw above that Meskill and Quah (2013) categorize research in terms of three distinct foci—online environments, socioaffective dimensions, and pedagogical processes—which, they suggest, 'may assist researchers in being clear and consistently explicit about the purposes and perspectives of their studies' (2014, p. 52). This is a reasonable claim, given that their three foci are likely to remain present in online mediated language learning, even with future—and as yet unknown—developments in technology.

There are other ways to categorize the research; the 'historical' perspectives of Warschauer and Bax have already been mentioned in Chapter 1. A related way of making sense of CALL research is to take a technology- or tools-based historical perspective (for example, Levy & Stockwell, 2006; Hubbard, 2009). This view traces the development of specific technologies, from the earliest uses of computers in tutorial CALL providing drills and text-reconstruction activities, through multimedia CD-ROMs providing content and being used to teach culture, up to the more recent developments in Web 2.0 tools and including social networks, gaming, and virtual worlds, as well as mobile technologies.

A language skills approach can also be used to categorize research (see, for example, Ducate & Arnold, 2006; Hubbard, 2009). This involves looking at the separate language skills—speaking, listening, reading, writing, grammar, vocabulary, and pronunciation, as well as cultural and intercultural competence—and organizing research within these categories. This is one approach that speaks particularly to teachers, as they are often working with classes that focus on one or two skills, for example teaching writing or reading. Even in classes that follow an **integrated skills approach**, such as that reflected in many EFL coursebooks, the language skills are often presented separately; teachers can fairly easily relate to research that looks at technology being used to enhance a specific skill, for example, the use of blogs to develop students' writing. Indeed, many methodology handbooks on how to integrate technology into the language classroom— both face to face and online—are divided into sections relating to language skills and offer practical activities for each skill (see, for example, Hockly & Clandfield, 2010; Stanley, 2013). The language skills approach will be used to categorize the research with young learners and adolescents described in Chapters 3 and 4.

Summary

The deployment of technologies in education is closely related to their use and status in wider society, and to the perceived benefits that they can bring to learning. The hype and hope surrounding the use of learning technologies, frequently tied to economic and political interests, needs to be counterbalanced by an awareness of what the research actually says about the effectiveness of hardware and software in school settings. Although school-age learners appear to be glued to digital devices on an almost permanent basis, at least in their out-of-school lives, the digital divide still persists between—and within—a wide variety of contexts and environments. The myth of the digital native still has much traction in wider society, despite research showing that 'younger' does not necessarily mean 'better' or more effective when it comes to using new technologies.

Research on learning technologies, most of which has taken place within the CALL research tradition, is a thriving academic field influenced by a number of theoretical frameworks and research perspectives. We will keep all of this mind as we turn to examine this research in more detail in Chapters 3 and 4.

3

Learning Technologies Research and Young Learners

Preview

In Chapter 2, we reviewed some of the wider concepts related to the role of learning technologies in education, and saw that this is not a straightforward matter. It is often an arena for highly charged debates that mix politics, economic interests, and beliefs about teaching and learning. In the first part of this chapter, we continue to examine wider concepts relevant to the role of technology in primary education. We consider key issues such as support for learners with special educational needs and e-safety—electronic or online safety, in each case referring to relevant research. We also examine the One Laptop per Child (OLPC) initiative, which is frequently aimed at primary school students and has been implemented in several countries. We take a critical look at the successes and failures of this initiative as reflected in the research, and consider what this might mean for the drive towards technology adoption in primary schools around the world.

In the second half of this chapter, we look more specifically at research studies examining the extent to which learning technologies can support second and foreign language learning in primary school classrooms.

Activity 3.1

Drawing on your experience and that of others, answer these questions:

- Are issues such as children spending too much time in front of screens relevant to teachers?
- Can technology support language learners with special educational needs?
- Can technology increase students' motivation and engagement with learning materials?
- Can technology help students develop individual language skills, for example reading, writing, speaking, and listening?
- Can technologies designed for older users, such as social networking sites and virtual worlds, have a place in the primary classroom?

Keep your answers in mind as you read this chapter.

Young Learners and Technology

Children of different ages are at very different stages of physical, conceptual, emotional, and cognitive development. Even within the same age group they are at different stages. When we talk about using learning technologies with primary school children, we need to keep in mind the widely varying needs, abilities, and experiences between age groups and between individuals. When working with technology in the classroom, young children with developing cognitive and motor skills need to use simple computer programs that are suited to their stage of development. For example, a kindergarten-aged child can easily tap on a mobile device screen in response to an audio prompt, so a suitable activity for a kindergarten-aged EFL learner might involve listening to a vocabulary word and tapping on the corresponding picture from a selection on the screen. Older primary school children who are able to read and write can be expected to use programs that are more demanding both linguistically and conceptually—for example, a story-telling app that requires them to interact with a text not only by tapping on the screen but also by responding verbally to prompts written in the story. Clearly, choosing computer programs or mobile apps that match the stage of development of a child is important. However, there are also wider social issues at play in the use of technology with primary school students, and we discuss some of these below.

Screen Time

Some of the fears about technology in wider society that we identified at the beginning of Chapter 1 take on a particular sense of urgency when considering children. Concerns about children spending too much time on digital devices—'screen time'—and becoming overdependent on these devices are very real for many teachers and parents. In developed countries such as the USA, where access to cell phones, tablets, and laptops is fairly ubiquitous, even very young children can spend several hours a day looking at electronic screens. However, because parents are usually in control of the content on digital devices, younger children are frequently viewing what their parents consider to be educational content. As children get older, though, the amount of educational content they view decreases. A US-based study by the Joan Ganz Cooney Center, a non-profit research institute, interviewed 1,577 parents online and found that two- to four-year-olds spent just over two hours a day on screen time—including watching television—with one hour and 16 minutes of this spent on educational content (Rideout, 2014). The ratio of educational content was different for older children: the study found that eight- to ten-year-olds spent more than two and a half hours a day on screen time but that only 42 minutes of this was considered educational (Rich, 2014). Nevertheless, as psychologist Aric Sigman points out:

> irrespective of the content or educational value of what is being viewed, the sheer amount of average daily screen time during discretionary hours after school is increasingly being considered an independent risk factor for disease, and is recognised as such by other governments and medical bodies.
>
> (Sigman, 2012, no page number)

In some Asia-Pacific countries—for example, Singapore, China, and South Korea—concerns over children's dependency on digital devices has led to the establishment of internet addiction treatment centers. The extent to which 'internet addiction' is a medical disorder is contentious, but there is no doubt that pediatricians, such as those of the American Academy of Pediatrics, and advocacy groups, such as the Alliance for Childhood, urge caution over exposing very young children to an excessive use of digital media. Research has shown that screen time has no real benefits for children under two years old; for children over three, some well-designed educational content can contribute to learning, especially when an adult is actively involved in mediating that content. However, some digital content can have very negative effects on children. For example, media violence, such as that found in some video games, has been linked to aggression, desensitization to violence, and a lack of empathy, as well as to poor school performance (Linn, 2012). A report by the Alliance for Childhood summarizes this research and adds that:

> [e]xtensive screen time is linked to a host of problems for children including childhood obesity, sleep disturbance, and learning, attention, and social problems. And time with screens takes away from other activities known to be more beneficial to their growth and development.
>
> (Alliance for Childhood, 2012, p. 5)

Despite concerns over screen time and its effect on early childhood, parents tend to feel that their own children are not at risk or that these risks apply to other people's children rather than their own (Plowman & McPake, 2013; Takeuchi, 2011). As Funk, Brouwer, Curtiss, and McBroom (2009) point out, media researchers seem to be more concerned about technology dominating children's lives than their parents are.

Nevertheless, faced with the research discussed above, the extent to which kindergarten and primary school children are exposed to use of devices in the classroom—for example, how many school hours are spent on devices and what educational content is included on these devices—is clearly an important issue. As any educator working with young children knows, exploring and learning via touch, sound, smell, and taste is vitally important for children's development, so replacing kinesthetic and experiential learning activities with computer software is clearly not an advisable way forward for teaching young children.

E-safety

Another area of concern for parents and teachers of young children is that of e-safety—that is, how to keep children safe online. The most common risks to children online are perceived to be **cyberbullying**; accessing inappropriate materials, such as violent content; the invasion of privacy and oversharing of personal information; and communicating with strangers online, also referred to as 'stranger danger'. Media hype does nothing to quell these fears (boyd, 2014).

Children in many countries have increasing access to devices and the internet, so attention in education has shifted to how to empower children to deal with online risks and to ensure that their uses of technology take place in safe environments as far as possible. Along with a focus on ICT skills, computer skills and/or digital literacies in the curriculum, many nationwide educational policies require primary—and secondary—schools to have e-safety policies and strategies in place. For example, since 2009, Ofsted (the Office for Standards in Education, Children's Services and Skills, the regulatory body in the UK that inspects schools), has required schools to demonstrate robust e-safety practices, including training in safe and responsible online behavior for students, and training for teachers in how best to support this (Shipton, 2011). Rather than banning access to the internet within schools or severely restricting access, there has been a gradual move towards the promotion of safe online practices, starting at primary level. This approach is seen as more realistic and, indeed, useful; in the words of Byron:

> simply blocking children and young people's access to the internet in schools … meant that they weren't able to access a range of sites that were beneficial for learning, and that they were less likely to develop the understanding of digital safety that they needed to be digitally safe outside of school.

(Byron, 2010, p. 16)

Whether a country has national e-safety policy guidelines, or whether individual states, districts, or schools are encouraged to develop their own e-safety policies, one thing is clear: children are using technology from ever younger ages, and schools increasingly feel the need to cater for this by ensuring that children learn about safe online practices.

Special Educational Needs and Assistive Technologies

One particularly promising way in which technology can be used with children is in supporting those with special educational needs (SEN). SEN has received much attention within mainstream schooling; however, there are far fewer studies available in the area of SEN and English language learning. In addition, in some cases, limited English proficiency can be erroneously diagnosed as limited learning ability, leading students to be wrongly placed in special education classes rather than given the language support they need (Lightbown, 2014). A report released by the Institute of Education Sciences in the USA examined how states deal with identifying and supporting ELLs with disabilities and found that:

> no proven method exists for identifying an English-learner student who has a learning disability and then placing the student in the most appropriate instructional program.
>
> (Burr, Haas, & Ferriere, 2015, p. 1)

Furthermore, the report found that the complex variables involved in trying to identify such a learner meant that there is 'evidence of English-learner students being both over- and under-represented in special education programs' (Burr, Haas, & Ferriere, 2015, p. 1).

Although a detailed consideration of SEN is beyond the scope of this volume, in this section we review some of the research into SEN and language learning, with a specific look at how technology can assist some SEN learners. We need to keep in mind that the term 'special education' covers a very wide range of needs, from children with mild dyslexia or mild intellectual disability through to severe learning difficulties and autism. It includes children with ADHD (attention deficit hyperactivity disorder), with visual or hearing impairments, or with mobility issues, restricted movement, and motor skills challenges. Clearly, each of these children has vastly differing needs and requires very different levels of support. Often children with milder disabilities are integrated into mainstream schooling—a so-called inclusive approach—and they may also have separate support or 'pull out' classes. The inclusive approach to SEN can pose challenges for teachers.

Unless specially trained, teachers are often unsure of how to meet their SEN children's emotional, functional, and academic needs (Mueller, Singer, & Carranza, 2006).

Mobile technology devices—especially tablets—have been praised for providing new and enhanced opportunities for technology-assisted learning for SEN children. Tablets have been enthusiastically taken up by many SEN educators and, indeed, the initial results seem promising. The assistive features of tablets are clearly of potential benefit for a range of SEN learners, both children and adults. For example:

- font size on a tablet can be easily increased
- screen contrast can be changed, or background and text colors can be reversed to help those with visual impairments
- audio capabilities can be turned on with text so that dyslexic students have the option of listening to a text rather than reading it
- subtitles and closed captions can be turned on for audio and video content and the size and font of these changed so that students with hearing impairments can read content
- sound settings on tablets include a mono option for students who have better hearing in one ear
- hearing aids can connect to some tablets via **Bluetooth**
- tactile screen settings can be changed from swipe movements to tapping movements for students with motor skills challenges
- the motion of the interface can be reduced
- the screen display can be locked into one position so that screen movement is further reduced
- **assistive touch** on some tablets can help teachers guide students' reading around a screen.

Several research studies show that the assistive features of mobile technology can improve access and support learning for people with a range of disabilities. For example, text messaging can benefit people with hearing impairments (Voosloo, 2012); video messaging can enable sign language users to effectively communicate via technology (Ring & LaMarche, 2012); and the tactile interface and immediate sensory feedback of tablets can improve communication for autistic students in the classroom (Johnson, Adams, & Cummins, 2012). A study in Australia found that multimodal texts created for tablets and laptops were successful in supporting the literacy development of two autistic children, one aged five and the other aged eight (Oakley, Howitt, Garwood, & Durack, 2013). In general, research seems to suggest that within mainstream education the multimodal and tactile assistive qualities of tablets have the potential to increase SEN learners' engagement, develop their academic and communicative skills, and improve social interaction (Campigotto, McEwen, & Demmans Epp, 2013; Kagohara et al., 2013).

Apart from the built-in assistive features of tablets, there is also a wide range of educational apps available for SEN learners, from **text-to-speech** and **speech-to-text** apps to simple writing apps that can help them learn to spell letters by tracing them on a touch screen. Meanwhile, more sophisticated apps enable teachers to create video scenarios for their SEN students in order to develop empathy and social skills. There are also organizations that provide documentation and lesson plans that can help teachers work with SEN students in the language classroom, for example Languages Without Limits and the Training and Development Agency for Schools in the UK.

Given the potential, how, then, can tablet technology support SEN learners who are also English language learners? Classroom Snapshot 3.1 below provides one example.

Classroom Snapshot 3.1

Four ELL elementary school students with language-based disabilities, all aged seven or eight, are taking part in a language arts class in a school in Northern California, USA. All four students have Spanish as their home language and none has used a tablet before. Each child is sitting with an iPad and wearing headphones. They are using a preloaded application called Language Builder and are working at their own pace. The app shows the student a picture. A voice prompt asks the student to make a sentence about the picture and to include certain words in the sentence. The student records a sentence in the app before playing the sentence back to listen to it. The student then moves on to the next picture and repeats the process. The students use this app regularly in the language arts class over a period of six weeks. In the beginning, the students are very engaged in the activities and this engagement increases during the first four lessons; however, over time, their engagement with the learning materials decreases, and the teacher needs to prompt them more often to continue working with the app.

(Cumming & Draper Rodriguez, 2013)

This study aimed to determine the impact of using tablet technology—in this case iPads—on these SEN learners' academic engagement in language arts lessons. In addition, the study measured the satisfaction of the teachers and learners in using the tablet technology. The baseline phase of the study consisted of students completing sentence formation activities, both written and oral, which were similar to the Language Builder activities but took place with no technology.

The results of the study showed that all four SEN students learned new vocabulary using the app. It also found that the learners' academic engagement increased during the first four lessons; engagement was measured by the number of prompts that the teacher needed to give individual students to keep them on task. However, their engagement decreased towards the end of the study, although the number of prompts needed to keep the students on task was never as high as those needed in the baseline non-technology phase. The learners themselves reported feeling that they had learned new language but also getting bored with the app after a time; the researchers suggested that this may have been because the novelty of using the iPad had worn off and the task was fairly repetitive. They also suggested that the lack of feedback in the app may not have reinforced the content enough for the students and that the students may have grown bored as they became more proficient in the task of formulating sentences. A major advantage reported by the teachers in this study was that it enabled the SEN students to work independently. As suggested by the researchers, a longer time period for a study such as this, involving more students and a variety of apps in different subject areas, would provide a fruitful basis for further research.

Implementing Technology in Primary Schools

In the 1980s and 1990s, if computers were to be found in schools at all, they were typically kept in large computer rooms—also known as computer labs—where English language students might be taken once or twice a week to use specialized language learning software (see Chapter 1). However, the decreasing cost of hardware has meant that many schools, in both developing and developed countries, are now able to implement technology in a range of ways.

One Laptop per Child

Launched in 2005, the One Laptop per Child (OLPC) initiative is the brainchild of Nicholas Negroponte. It initially aimed to provide cheaply produced XO laptops—informally known as the '100-dollar laptop'—to 100–150 million primary school students in the world's poorest countries by 2008, although to date this goal has not been met. The OLPC initiative has been implemented in several countries to support English language learning alongside other school subjects. Although not restricted to primary school students, OLPC tends to be implemented first with the primary school age group and then expanded to secondary school students—as in the case of the OLPC *Conectar Igualdad* program in Argentina, among others.

The OLPC initiative has been lauded and criticized in equal measure. It has been praised for its social justice agenda and attempts to provide access to education, via technology, to the world's poorest children, especially in areas where access to trained teachers is difficult or non-existent. Yet it has been scorned for the techno-solutionism that underpins the belief that, simply by putting hardware into the hands of children, quality learning will ensue.

There is no doubt that the OLPC project is a radical and innovative one in many ways, but the principles of OLPC have been taken on board by many governments worldwide with mixed results. As was the case with IWBs (see Chapter 2), a belief that educational challenges can be solved through hardware has turned out to be misguided. For example, an OLPC initiative in Peru, launched in 2007 with 290,000 laptops supplied to primary school children, soon ran into infrastructure problems. Access to electricity and to the internet proved patchy, and despite student and teacher enthusiasm for the project, a lack of technical support and a lack of pedagogical training for teachers seriously hampered early efforts in the program (Warschauer & Ames, 2010; Trucano, 2012).

There are several reasons why OLPC has frequently proved less than successful. The techno-solutionist view has meant that vital factors such as necessary technical infrastructure—access to Wi-fi, or even to electricity—and educational infrastructure—such as appropriate curricula, materials, and teacher training—have either been pushed into the background or not considered at all. There has often been little or no regard for local context or the appropriacy of materials preloaded onto the laptops. For example, in Ethiopia and India, Eurocentric English language learning materials have been included on the XO laptops, leading to accusations of educational colonialism (Clark, 2013; Selwyn, 2013). Overall, sustainability has been low on the agenda of OLPC initiatives. There has been a tendency towards nationwide rollouts rather than a staged approach starting with smaller-scale pilot studies that are carefully evaluated. The low-cost XO laptops created for OLPC have proved to be less durable than expected, unreliable, and fraught with hardware and software issues. In addition, governments cannot always afford to supply laptops to all schoolchildren in the countries targeted; even if the initial cost per laptop is around 100 dollars, budgets to maintain and repair the laptops can be unsustainably high for low-income countries. As pointed out by Warschauer and Ames (2010), these countries 'would be better off building schools, training teachers, developing curricula, providing books and subsidizing attendance' (p. 34)—measures which research has shown to improve learning outcomes in the world's poorer countries.

Nevertheless, when a more considered, strategic approach to the rollout of an OLPC project is taken, results can be encouraging. Uruguay is one such example. The Uruguayan OLPC initiative is called *Plan Ceibal*, and it has an overt social justice agenda based on equality, learning, and technology. One part of the project, *Ceibal en Inglés* (Ceibal in English), aims to bring English language learning to all primary students in the country. Facing a chronic shortage of trained and proficient English language teachers, *Ceibal en Inglés* uses videoconferencing to digitally project trained English teachers into classrooms around the country. Classroom Snapshot 1.2 in Chapter 1 describes a typical *Ceibal en Inglés* class. The project has deliberately tried to avoid making the same mistakes as previous OLPC initiatives (Stanley, 2015). With an emphasis on reliable hardware and infrastructure, the project integrates culturally appropriate English language learning materials specially created for Uruguayan primary school children, includes strong online and face-to-face teacher training programs, and offers continued post-training support for teachers by specialized mentors. Although the relatively small size of Uruguay's population—around 3.5 million—has undoubtedly helped in achieving a nationwide rollout of *Plan Ceibal*, the success of *Ceibal en Inglés* is in no small part also due to a staged rollout over several years. Pilot phases have been evaluated, and adjustments to hardware, learning materials, and training made as necessary. Initial impact studies of *Ceibal en Inglés* are encouraging (Banegas, 2013; Brovetto, in press), with children involved in the program showing clear signs of progress in English language learning (Woods, 2014). (For more on *Ceibal en Inglés,* see Brovetto, in press, and Stanley, 2015.)

One-to-One Initiatives in North America

The idea of providing one laptop for every child has not been restricted to developing countries. Developed countries, too, have implemented educational policies at national, state, district, or school level that attempt to put laptops—or increasingly, these days, tablets—into the hands of students of all ages. These are frequently referred to as one-to-one or 1:1 initiatives, meaning one device for one student.

Some of the more ill-conceived of these one-to-one programs have come across the same challenges as the OLPC initiative. For example, the mayor and the president of the City Council of Birmingham County, Alabama, USA, introduced an OLPC initiative with XO laptops in 2009. This was done despite strong resistance from school district officials who were concerned about the lack of internet access in most Birmingham elementary schools, as well as a lack of funding for curriculum development and teacher training. After a short six-week pilot program in one school, 15,000 XO laptops were distributed to children in elementary schools in the district. This particular OLPC initiative soon ran into many of the issues that beset one-to-one programs when they are introduced too quickly and without thought to the necessary infrastructure. For example, 70 percent of the laptops had technical problems in the first six months, over 80 percent of the students used the XO laptops very infrequently in school, teachers were uninterested and uninvolved in the initiative, and internet access was either non-existent or unreliable (Warschauer & Ames, 2010; Warschauer, 2011). In addition, most students in Birmingham County already had access to computers outside of school, but after receiving the XO laptops, students' use of those computers for academic or content creation purposes decreased, while their use of the XO laptops for chat room communication and instant messaging increased. Also, students' anxiety with computers increased after receiving the XO laptops, and the percentage of students who reportedly wanted to attend college decreased. The cost of the program increased significantly over time, as students graduated or moved away with the laptops, or laptops were broken, lost, or misplaced (Warschauer, Cotton, & Ames, 2012). Overall, the Birmingham OLPC program illustrates the more widespread problem of:

> putting great faith in the power of technology to bring about
> improvement and insufficient attention to the surrounding factors
> needed to make technology successful.

> (Warschauer, 2011, p. 5)

Nevertheless, just as there are successful implementations of OLPC programs in developing countries like Uruguay, so too are there success stories of one-to-one initiatives in developed countries. Spotlight Study 3.1 describes one of these.

Spotlight Study 3.1

Littleton School District in Colorado, USA, launched a one-to-one laptop program in 2008–2009, as part of a new district curricular initiative for improving writing and literacy called the Universal Literacy Framework. A particular need for supporting literacy development was identified at the district's special school for English language learners—who made up 70 percent of the school population—where the program focused on developing students' writing skills through the use of blogs, wikis, and social media. The program included professional development for principals and teachers to help them understand the nature of the new curriculum and how technology could support this through an increased emphasis on student writing. The hardware and software for the project were chosen to fit the curricular objectives: a low-cost **netbook**, or small laptop, with **open source software**, and free cloud-based online resources rather than commercial educational software, which is often expensive. A pilot program was carried out in the first year with the fifth-grade students in the district and evaluated; after this, the program was expanded to sixth- and ninth-grade students and evaluated at the end of the second year. Evaluation of these pilot stages found improved test scores and an enthusiastic response to the initiative from teachers and students, and subsequently the program was expanded to all students between fifth and tenth grades. The success of Littleton's one-to-one program rests on the fact that a range of key factors was taken into account in the design and implementation of the program. For example, training was provided to teachers, reliable hardware was purchased, and the necessary technical infrastructure to support the program was put in place in schools. In addition, the pilot stages were evaluated before the initiative was rolled out to the whole district.

(Warschauer, 2011) ■

More recently, many one-to-one initiatives have favored tablets over laptops, citing reasons of portability, affordability and ubiquitous access, improved internet coverage, and the potential for more individualized and personalized learning experiences (Melhuish & Falloon, 2010). One-to-one mobile device initiatives in North America are generally school- or district-led and frequently implemented with the overt pedagogical aim of supporting and enhancing learning. Three broad approaches can be identified: schools provide the devices; BYOD initiatives, in which students use their own mobile devices in and out of school; and shared expense plans, where the cost of devices and broadband access is shared between the ᵖlans, where the cost of devices and broadband access is shared between the ᵖarents via leasing options or parental contributions (Fritschi).

In Canada, provincial governments (for example, Alberta Government, 2012, 2013; Government of Saskatchewan, 2013) provide guidelines for schools wishing to integrate the use of mobile devices to enhance learning, although large-scale province-wide initiatives are rare to date. Nonetheless, one notable initiative in Ontario, the L4All K–12 Regional Project, was launched by the Rainbow District School Board in 2011, with a pilot phase in which tablets were provided to volunteer Grade 9 teachers in the district, working with 35 students. During the academic year of 2012–2013, 1,000 students worked with the tablets; this included SEN students who worked with individual educational plans on the tablets as part of the Assistive Technology Learning Community. An evaluation of this initiative (Wachnuk, 2013) found gains in literacy for students using the tablets, and especially for the SEN students following individual learning plans.

In the United States, several school district one-to-one initiatives with tablets have been undertaken at primary and secondary level. For example, the Dodge City Public School District in Kansas, the Eloy Elementary School District in Arizona, and the Coachella Valley Unified School District in California all started one-to-one tablet initiatives with pilot programs in 2013, followed by wider rollouts in 2014. Nevertheless, evaluations of the effectiveness of tablet deployment in initiatives like this are still thin on the ground. This is true of initiatives both in North America and internationally. For example, a 2015 Commonwealth of Learning report on government-sponsored tablet initiatives around the world found that many of the reasons for investing in these initiatives rested on 'catchphrases and buzzwords that may have been more fitting for public relations and political campaigns than for educational reform actions' (Tamim, Borokhovski, Pickup, & Bernard, 2015, p. 23).

One-to-one programs require substantial funding for infrastructure, hardware, and software. This means that school districts can come under pressure from educational technology vendors. What is more, educational technology purchases in schools and districts are often made without consideration for the end users—essentially students and teachers—as vendors pitch their hardware and software products to district supervisors and school managers (Cuban, 2015c). Concerns such as these may appear at first blush to be irrelevant to the realm of learning technologies research and may feel far removed from the concerns of purely academic studies; however, this is wishful thinking. Wider political and economic decisions impact on what technologies are deployed in the classroom and on what learning materials are chosen for students to work with, and these then often set research agendas. Indeed, research can help uncover the effectiveness or otherwise of learning technologies policy and purchasing decisions by looking at what actually happens in classrooms and asking what, if any, learning results. In the case of larger one-to-one initiatives, both in North America and elsewhere, this is still an under-researched area, although some initial reports reviewing research on iPads in the classroom are encouraging, as we see in Spotlight Study 3.2.

Spotlight Study 3.2

In a report reviewing one-to-one iPad implementations, mainly in the UK but also internationally, Clark and Luckin (2013) identified several benefits for students and teachers. For example, many of the iPad projects reviewed in the report showed how tablets could promote seamless learning—that is, learning across formal classroom contexts and informal, personal, and social contexts; the tactile interface motivated and engaged students; the devices enabled learning to be enhanced in ways that were not previously possible; taking devices home improved home–school communication; and the devices could work in combination with other technologies and create learning data that could be used for reflection, assessment, and evaluation. Nevertheless, the researchers pointed to the importance for schools of having a clear rationale for their iPad implementation as well as the need for long-term planning before, during, and after rollout. Reliable infrastructure and technical support were also found to be crucial to successful implementation, as was the involvement of all the stakeholders, including parents. ■

Learning Technologies Research with Primary School Learners

In this section of the chapter, we examine research that has attempted to evaluate the use and effectiveness of learning technologies in second language teaching and learning. However, this is no straightforward task. The fundamental aims in research studies can vary significantly. To understand this difference, Ware and Hellmich (2014) draw a helpful distinction between learning technologies studies that focus on *learning outcomes* and studies that focus on *learning opportunities*. Outcomes-focused studies attempt to identify to what extent technologies might lead to specific measurable gains in second language learning. As such, they tend to be more narrowly focused and to rely mainly on **quantitative research** methods. Opportunities-focused studies are more exploratory in nature and attempt to gauge to what extent technologies might support language learning in a more general sense—for example, by providing increased opportunities for language practice in informal out-of-school contexts. As such, researchers in these studies tend to take a wider—often sociolinguistic or ecological—perspective and to rely mainly on **qualitative research** methods. Of course, these research orientations are not mutually exclusive, and one can find studies in which both research approaches can be identified.

When reviewing research studies into learning technologies and language learning, we also need to keep in mind that what may be a successful small-scale research project in one context may be less successful in another context. In a world of increasingly complex technologies being used in increasingly complex environments and interactions, it becomes difficult to say that technology x will always produce language learning result y; the range of factors involved in any learning situation is simply too varied. As Thomas et al. point out, it is important to realize that:

> merely referencing success with small-scale projects and arguing that they can be generalized and applied in uniform ways across language learning environments is no longer feasible. CALL technologies do not provide a panacea for all of the challenges facing language learners and educators; integration cannot be seamless, nor can it be applied by all language educators in all contexts.
>
> (Thomas et al., 2013, p. 8)

In addition, not all research studies are firmly grounded in theory. For example, in a review of 43 empirical research studies into Web 2.0 tools in a number of learning technology journals and books, Wang and Vásquez (2012) found that over half of the studies—56 percent—did not have an identifiable theoretical foundation. They also found that several of the studies suffered from common methodological weaknesses, such as **convenience sampling** of participants, rather than **random sampling** or **purposeful sampling**. They pointed out that in K–12 contexts, this was often due to logistical issues such as controlled access to minors or the need to work with already formed groups of students in individual classrooms. Wang and Vásquez also identified a general shift in these research studies from primarily quantitative approaches to data collection to an emphasis on qualitative data. However, they pointed out that some research studies failed to carry out in-depth analyses of qualitative data, such as exploring students' perspectives to help explain observed phenomena. Another weakness they identified stemmed from the techno-centric view taken by some researchers, in which the technology alone was held to account for learning, without consideration for the wider pedagogical context—such as teaching strategies or instructional materials.

With these caveats in mind, we will examine both small-scale research studies and larger studies. As we will see, in some cases research findings point to measurable gains in language learning, while in other cases, results are mixed. As we have discussed previously in this volume, comparing the results of research studies is problematic, even when a single technology, such as cell phones, or a single tool, such as blogs, is used, given the wide range of contextual factors involved in learning that go well beyond the technology in question. Also, given the scope of this volume, we need to limit our review of learning technologies research to a number of key or significant examples, so for each of the research areas identified in this section, we look at two or three studies. Nevertheless, by reviewing a range of studies, we hope to give the reader an understanding of the different research approaches, agendas, and tools that make up the rich body of learning technologies research.

We divide this section into research studies that focus on vocabulary acquisition, followed by studies that address the four skills: reading, writing, listening, and speaking. We choose this division for the studies because researchers themselves are often concerned with exploring gains in these specific language areas. We finish the section by taking a brief look at newer online spaces for collaboration, such as virtual worlds, and what this might mean for primary school students' language acquisition.

Research into Vocabulary Acquisition

As with the majority of learning technologies research, most of the studies into vocabulary acquisition have taken place in secondary school and university contexts. However, there is some research into vocabulary acquisition with younger students, particularly with mobile devices. As cell phones, **smartphones**, and tablets become increasingly available and affordable, and with their rich multimedia capabilities and additional features such as **GPS tracking**, some recent studies have examined how these devices might support vocabulary acquisition for primary school students. Generally speaking, research into language acquisition with mobile devices can be divided into two categories: *content-based* research and *design-oriented* research (Kukulska-Hulme & Shield, 2007). Content-based research focuses on digital content that is delivered via mobile devices, whereas design-oriented research examines the learning experience that can be facilitated by the use of a mobile device, often in out-of-class socially oriented contexts. The portability of mobile devices means that they can easily be used both inside and outside the classroom, providing opportunities for learners to take part in language learning tasks in informal, real-life contexts—often referred to as 'situated' learning contexts.

Because **lexis** can provide a finite set of items for students to acquire, several research studies into the use of mobile devices to support vocabulary acquisition take a content-based approach, with words or idioms presented to students via the devices, for example as key words, phrases, or quizzes, possibly in the form of flashcards or regular SMS messages. Students' acquisition of the lexis is then tested (for example, see studies with adults by Thornton & Houser, 2002; Levy & Kennedy, 2005; see also our review of content-based vocabulary studies based on SMS messages with secondary school students in Chapter 4). In contrast to this approach, a design-oriented study examining how vocabulary learning can be supported by the use of mobile devices in a primary school is described in Classroom Snapshot 3.2.

Classroom Snapshot 3.2

Forty eight-year-old primary school students in Singapore are learning six English prepositions of place—'above', 'below', 'next to', etc.—in an EFL class. Once the teacher has presented the new language to the students, they are given cell phones and they move around the school grounds taking photos of real-life objects or situations in which these prepositions of place are illustrated. For example, they take photos of objects next to each other, or they position classmates next to each other, or above or below objects. The students return to the classroom and share their photos with classmates, describing each photo and using the prepositions of place to do so. Finally, the students complete a paper-based worksheet, in which they need to show their understanding of the six prepositions.

(Wong & Looi, 2010)

In this study, Wong and Looi (2010) aimed to recreate the three essential stages necessary for vocabulary acquisition as defined by Nation (2001): noticing a new item, retrieval of the new item by encountering it several times, and using the new item creatively in new contexts. They also wanted to explore the potential of cell phones to provide the students with opportunities to apply the vocabulary to new, real-world contexts. Rather than pushing pre-packaged learning content to the students via the devices, the phones were used as tools by the students themselves to create their own new sentences, via photos. Through an evaluation of the students' worksheets at the end of the class, it appeared that the students were able to use the prepositions successfully. Nevertheless, the very short nature of this intervention—a single class—and the need for additional testing on the ability of these students to retrieve the prepositions at a later date suggest that this sort of intervention would benefit from a longer time frame. Nevertheless, it provides an interesting example of a design-led mobile-based intervention, in which the technology is seen as a tool to create learner-centered additional learning opportunities outside of the classroom.

A research study that took place within a longer time frame and that combines a content-based and design-oriented approach was carried out by Sandberg, Maris, and de Geus (2011) with fifth-grade students at three different schools in the Netherlands. The study compared the use of mobile devices out of the class to support vocabulary acquisition with a paper-based in-school-only control group. All the students were given a classroom lesson about zoo animals and were then divided into three groups: a control group of 29 students and two experimental groups of 24 and 22 students respectively. The two experimental groups then visited a zoo and used smartphones with a preloaded app to guide their zoo visit. The app used GPS tracking to guide the children to different animals during the zoo visit and provided information on each animal in context. The experimental group of 24 students had access to the smartphones only while at the zoo; the second experimental group of 22 students were allowed to take the phones home for two weeks and had access to a set of five additional games on the phones: a spelling quiz, a yes/no game, a memory game, a multiple-choice quiz, and a jigsaw puzzle. Once the student had chosen a game, the app played a short video about an animal and the student then needed to use the information in the video to successfully complete the game. Post-test scores on a 50-word vocabulary test showed gains in vocabulary acquisition for all the groups, with the students who took the mobile phones home performing best. However, there was no significant difference in post-test scores between the control group, who received classroom instruction only, and the experimental group who used the smartphones in the zoo but did not take them home. The researchers suggested that the additional time spent working with learning materials by the group who took the phones home—an average of an hour and a half per student—was the defining factor that improved their learning outcomes in this study. It appears that this group was motivated by the additional games in the app, but the researchers also reported that the amount of time students spent using the app significantly decreased over the two weeks, suggesting that as the novelty of the content wore off, motivation and engagement with the learning materials decreased. We saw a similar dip in motivation and engagement with computer-based learning materials in the section on SEN students earlier in this chapter: Classroom Snapshot 3.1 found that SEN students soon became bored with a fairly limited and repetitive multimedia exercise.

Motivation, it would seem, is a key element in keeping students engaged with learning content; these studies show that it is difficult to assert that multimedia content alone or the use of a specific technology device, however modern, will automatically lead to improved learning outcomes. A further example clearly illustrates this point: a study by Hung, Young, and Lin (2009) explored the effect on vocabulary acquisition of a crossword game played on a tablet compared to the same game played by students with pen and paper. In a class of 32 Taiwanese primary school EFL students, half the class used the tablets and the other half used pen and paper. The researchers found no significant differences between the two groups, although learning outcomes, motivation, and attitude improved for all the students and especially for lower-achieving students. In this case, the design of the activity—a crossword puzzle—appeared to be the main motivating factor that led to improved learning outcomes, not the tablet technology.

Research into Skills Development

In this section, we review a number of studies that focus on the acquisition of reading, writing, listening, and speaking skills, and the role that technology may play in supporting this for primary school learners. Some of the studies focus on a single skill, such as reading, while others focus on two or more skills. For example, if students use blogs to develop their writing skills, they are also working on their reading skills by reading and leaving written comments on their peers' blog posts. In cases like these, researchers often choose to focus on only one of the skills, for example writing blog posts, in an attempt to limit the focus of a study. In other studies, researchers might use tools that require students to listen and then speak; in a case like this, gains in both skills might be investigated.

Research into Early EFL Reading

We begin with research into how technology can be used to support primary-level students develop their early reading skills in a foreign language. This is challenging because young learners are still developing literacy and reading in their L1; it is doubly challenging if the learners' L1 uses a non-Roman script because the children also need to learn an additional writing system to be able to decipher English. Collaborative practices, such as reading in small groups, have been found to support the development of children's reading ability. A number of studies from Taiwan investigated how technology could be used to support both collaborative reading practices and basic reading skills such as phoneme and word recognition.

Lan, Sung, and Chang (2007) carried out two consecutive quasi-experimental studies with two classes of 26 third-grade primary school children in Taiwan to assess the impact on collaborative learning and early EFL reading of a mobile-device-based intervention. The first study attempted to identify weaknesses in collaborative learning during reading classes in the two primary school classes by video-recording the learners' interactions. In this first study, which lasted one ten-week semester, identical instructional materials were used, but one class, the experimental group, learned reading through a collaborative approach, while the second class, the control group, learned reading through individual study followed by whole-class activities led by the EFL instructor. The outcomes found that although some collaborative reading practices were identified in the experimental group, simply putting the students into small heterogeneous reading groups did not guarantee that group leaders were effective in supporting their peers. In a minority of the small groups, the leaders ignored those that needed help or taunted lower-proficiency students. In some groups, the leaders asked the medium-ability students to read alone while they helped less proficient classmates, leaving the medium-ability students confused or uncertain about the reading task.

The second study also lasted one semester and evaluated the use of a specially designed program for tablets called MPAL—Mobile-device-supported Peer-Assisted Learning—that was developed to address the weaknesses identified from the first study; in this second study, both classes of 26 students used MPAL. MPAL aimed to provide the students with the necessary scaffolding for individual reading when peers were not available and to provide group members with a simple way to support each other in reading. It consisted of two modules: a phonological skills training module to ensure students reached a certain standard in sight reading words, followed by a read-aloud module, in which students read longer texts to online helpers—peers—via Skype. If they passed this second module, they were eligible to become online helpers for other peers. The researchers found that using MPAL increased the students' motivation to learn and enhanced their oral reading confidence; it also reduced their stress with EFL reading and increased student collaboration in learning to read.

Lan, Sung, and Chang (2009) then went on to develop MPAL into a three-component mobile-based system for early EFL reading called CAREER (Computer-Assisted Reciprocal Early English Reading), which included a sight word module, a phonetic word module, and a peer assessment module. These three modules were based on what the researchers identified as three essential components for effective reading instruction: a balanced reading structure; immediate targeted feedback; and reciprocal or collaborative reading in small groups. A study was carried out over one semester with two classes of fourth-grade students in Taiwan: an experimental class of 26 students used CAREER and a control class of 26 students did not use the software. The researchers found that most students in the experimental group, including students of lower ability, showed gains in oral reading skills as well as improved reading comprehension. The experimental group also exhibited more effective collaborative work than the control group when completing specific reading tasks in small groups.

Lan, Sung, and Chang (2013) carried out a follow-up study with an adapted version of the CAREER system in one elementary school in Taiwan with 20 third-grade EFL students. Pre- and post-test scores showed significant gains in early reading abilities for these students, particularly in phoneme segmentation, in addition to increased positive attitudes towards learning English.

Research into Writing

Web 2.0 tools such as blogs and wikis have long been identified as potentially useful platforms for developing students' writing skills. Here, again, the majority of research has been carried out in university contexts and overall results appear encouraging (see Hourigan & Murray, 2010, for a review of research). There are a few examples of studies using blogs and wikis at primary school level and we examine some of these below. Other tools have been used to help develop students' writing too: for example, free online software to create graphic novels or cartoons, and tailor-made software delivering writing prompts to students via mobile devices.

We divide the writing research below into two sections: studies that have taken place in ESL contexts, such as the USA, and studies that have taken place in EFL contexts, such as Taiwan. Much of the research in ESL contexts takes place within the development of literacy, with ELLs working alongside native-speaker peers in English language arts classes. The research in EFL contexts takes place in a very different environment; like reading, writing in English is particularly challenging for primary students who use a different alphabet system in their first language.

Writing in ESL Contexts

Danzak (2011) describes a multimedia writing project called Graphic Journeys, which provided 32 English language learners at a middle school in Florida with the opportunity to share their and their families' stories as migrants to the USA in graphic novel format. The rationale for the writing project was based on the belief that:

> immigration narratives shape the identity of ELs [English learners] and constitute a compelling discourse that can provide a valuable linguistic resource [in the classroom].

(Danzak, 2011, p. 187)

During the project, the students read graphic novels, created journals, undertook interviews, and developed written texts with family photographs and other images as they created individual digital comics using the online tool Comic Life. According to Danzak, the project supported a multiliteracies pedagogy as students worked in various linguistic modalities, engaged in collaborative learning, and used visual and graphic arts to compose multimodal texts with technology. The project also showed a strong awareness of social context by providing traditionally disadvantaged students with an opportunity to explore and express their identity and cultural heritage as immigrants and to share these stories with others. The researcher claimed that the project acted as a multiliteracy bridge to academic literacy for these students, although there was no focus on measurable learning outcomes in the project.

Since the advent of Web 2.0, blogs have proved to be a popular tool among educators and researchers looking for ways to improve student writing, both in the L1 literacy classroom and in the EFL classroom (Blood, 2000; Winer, 2003). Although blogs—and wikis—have been more researched than other Web 2.0 tools, the majority of studies have taken place in university settings (Wang & Vásquez, 2012). Nevertheless, there are some blog studies that have been carried out with primary-level students. For example, Zheng and Warschauer's (2015) study described in Classroom Snapshot 1.3 shows one use of blogging as a tool to develop ELL primary students' writing skills in an L1 literacy classroom context. Blogging has been found to help develop primary school children's sense of writing for a wider audience, which, in turn, develops their writing skills and their writing confidence, as well as enabling them to connect their in-class experiences with learning opportunities outside the classroom (McGrail & Davis, 2011).

These findings are similar to those in a study by Gebhard, Shin, and Seger (2011) with a class of second-grade primary school ELLs in a high-poverty urban school in the USA. The study examined the use of a blog-mediated writing curriculum in the development of students' writing skills in different genres, for example reports and letters, over a period of 22 months. Of a total of 19 students in the class, 14 were Spanish-speaking ELLs and most were struggling to meet state writing and reading standards. Focusing on one student in the class, the researchers found that the blogging curriculum developed her writing skills, increased her confidence as a writer, and enabled her to interact in academic and social contexts by leaving blog comments on peers' work. It also improved her written language: she developed an ability to produce more complex linguistic structures, showed greater control over tense and modality, and demonstrated an improved understanding of the differences between spoken and written discourse.

Writing in EFL Contexts

Wikis have proved popular among teachers and researchers examining how Web 2.0 tools might support the development of writing skills. Much of the research into wikis emphasizes their potential for collaborative writing and for creating multiple drafts of written texts. As such, they are especially suited to **process approaches** to writing. Alias, DeWitt, Siraj, Kamaruddin, and Daud (2013) reviewed 49 research studies and articles about wikis written in six academic journals over a period of five years from 2007 to 2012 and mainly focused on adult learners. They found that wikis promoted learner engagement and collaborative learning, and that attitudes were generally positive towards wikis, although this depended on the teachers' and students' attitudes towards the tool, ease of access to the wiki, and effective task design (Guo & Stevens, 2011). They also suggested that future research into wikis should focus on students' perceptions of wikis within different cultures as well as the impact of different cultures on interaction patterns within wikis. For example, some research has found that students can be reluctant to edit or delete what another student has written (Yoo & Huang, 2011).

A small-scale wiki study carried out with a class of ten-year-old Primary Five EFL students in a Chinese primary school in Hong Kong reflects many of these findings (Woo, Chu, Ho, & Li, 2011). The researchers found that the affordances of a wiki helped scaffold students' writing during collaborative writing projects because the history/tracking function of the wiki provided the teacher with in-depth information about the types of edits the students were making. This enabled the teacher to offer support and feedback, thereby scaffolding the students' editing and writing process. The use of a wiki for writing was also perceived positively by the students, who felt it encouraged teamwork and improved their writing skills.

Another wiki study in four primary schools in Hong Kong, also with ten-year-old Primary Five EFL students, investigated the suitability of wikis as a platform for implementing inquiry project-based learning with students (Chu, Wong, Lee, Chow, & Ng, 2011). The students carried out an inquiry-based project on a wiki platform, and the effectiveness of the wiki was evaluated by means of an online questionnaire and group interviews. Four domains were evaluated: learning/pedagogy, motivation, group interaction, and technology. The researchers found that feedback was positive across all four domains; they concluded that the students enjoyed the learning experience and that their acquisition of knowledge and skills was enhanced by the use of the wiki.

These two wiki studies reflect the 'learning opportunities' approach we discussed earlier: the focus in the research is on exploring ways in which the use of certain tools in combination with effective tasks may provide opportunities for and support students' language development—in this case, students' writing skills. To complete this section on writing skills, we describe a research study that has a 'learning outcomes' orientation and in which the researchers measured specific gains in the development of students' writing through the implementation of specially created writing software installed on mobile phones.

Hwang et al. (2014) carried out a study at a middle school in Taiwan with two classes of sixth-grade EFL students. The study investigated the effect of providing writing support via mobile devices to help the students of one class—the experimental group—produce short written texts outside of the classroom. The writing support software encouraged the children to produce sentences in situated learning contexts and provided subject-related vocabulary words, help with sentence patterns, and the opportunity to take photos of the objects they were prompted to write about. The students could also read and comment on their peers' written texts. The texts produced by this experimental group were compared with writing produced by the other class—the control group—who received traditional classroom-based writing instruction. Significant gains in post-test scores for the experimental group suggested that providing writing support at the point of need—in the form of suggested vocabulary and example sentences—was highly effective; in addition, the writing prompts provided opportunities for students to memorize new vocabulary.

Activity 3.2

Imagine that you are teaching students aged 10–11 in a fifth-grade language arts class in a primary school in North America. More than half of your students are ELLs who are struggling to meet state standards in reading and writing. The ELLs come from a variety of backgrounds, although the majority are Spanish-speaking. What kinds of technology-based interventions could you design as the basis for a semester-long project to help all of your students develop their writing skills? For example, if you chose graphic novels, blogs, or wikis, what advantages or disadvantages might each technology have? How would the design of learning activities be affected by the technology chosen? How could you ensure that the ELLs in the class received the additional scaffolding and feedback needed to develop their writing skills? How might you evaluate any learning outcomes from the project?

Now imagine that you are teaching a class of 10- and 11-year-old EFL students in a context where English is a foreign language and where there is little or no use of English in the wider environment. Answer the above questions with this group of students in mind.

Research into Listening and Speaking

Listening and speaking skills often go together, and the first study described below examined both: in this case, listening to learning materials via mobile devices in a real-life setting led to students orally producing and sharing their own sentences.

Hwang and Chen (2013) carried out a research study with a group of 30 primary school EFL students in Taiwan, who used **PDAs** (**Personal Digital Assistants**) during their lunch hour at school, four days a week for two months. The PDAs were preloaded with multimedia learning materials that required the students to listen to content and record their reading of basic words, and then to complete simple sentences connected to their daily lunch menu. A control group studied food vocabulary and sentences in class with paper-based learning materials and without the support of PDAs. The researchers found that the experimental group using PDAs out of class significantly outperformed the control group learning in class and attributed this to the greatly increased opportunities for listening and speaking provided by the PDAs to the experimental group. As in the zoo study carried out in the Netherlands that we described earlier (Sandberg et al., 2011), one of the determining factors in enhancing these students' language acquisition appeared to be the extra time they spent listening to English and producing their own utterances. As in the zoo study, the mobile devices in this study provided students with extra opportunities for language practice in informal, out-of-class contexts.

Hwang and Chen's study provided primary students with very structured opportunities for speaking, albeit out of class. Extra unstructured speaking opportunities can be provided for students via synchronous online audio- or videoconferencing tools, such as Skype. By far the majority of research into these tools has been carried out in college and university contexts, for example in the kinds of studies we discussed in Chapter 2, where students take part in online cross-cultural exchange projects. Nevertheless, a qualitative study by Whyte (2011) in French primary schools followed six teachers during the first six months of a videoconferencing project with the aim of investigating how teacher cognition—that is, their beliefs about language teaching and learning—affected their use of the videoconferencing tool with students. Data were collected from students, teachers, and trainers via recordings of the videoconferencing sessions, audio recordings of feedback sessions, questionnaires, teacher and trainer discussions, and video-stimulated recall interviews. The study identified several different approaches and teaching strategies used by the different teachers, which affected the interaction patterns and learning opportunities afforded to the students during videoconferencing. The teachers were guided by general, rather than foreign-language-specific, pedagogical principles; for example, while in theory most teachers valued spontaneous interaction between the students as an important goal during videoconferencing sessions, filmed data of these revealed that few opportunities were provided for unplanned student-to-student interaction. The researcher suggested that these findings related to teachers' views of language as a product rather than a process; in practice, this meant that for the more learner-centered teachers in this study, spontaneity was limited by rehearsal, while for the more teacher-centered practitioners, student participation was limited by excessive teacher talking time. This study is a particularly clear example of how teacher beliefs will affect their pedagogical approach, which can result in differing ways of using exactly the same technology. This study shows us once again that frequently it is not the technology itself that determines learning outcomes or opportunities but rather the way it is interpreted and implemented by teachers.

Communicating in Online Social Spaces: Virtual Worlds

As we saw in Chapters 1 and 2, the 'social turn' (Block, 2003) in second language acquisition research, coupled with the development of Web 2.0 tools, has resulted in an increased interest in how interaction with others online can support language learning. In secondary and adult language learning contexts, social networking sites, virtual worlds, and online games are some of the newer arenas that can promote online interaction. However, because of age restrictions and concerns over e-safety, these types of sites are often considered less suitable for primary school children. Nevertheless, there has been some fruitful recent research into the use of online virtual worlds with primary school students learning English, and it has been focused on learning outcomes and learning opportunities. In Spotlight Study 3.3, the researchers were very aware of issues of appropriacy and e-safety, so access to the virtual world in this study (Second Life) was carefully restricted and controlled by the teacher.

Spotlight Study 3.3

Sadler and Dooly (2014) carried out an ethnographic research project funded by the Spanish Ministry of Education in the 3D virtual world Second Life, with a group of six-year-old beginner EFL students in a school in Catalonia, Spain, and a group of eight-year-old L1-English-speaking learners studying language arts in a school in Ontario, Canada. The aims of the project were to examine to what extent collaboration between the two classes, including in the 3D world, might help these students develop their linguistic/communicative, digital, artistic, and intercultural competences. The main online activities were divided into three consecutive phases. In the first phase, the students recorded and edited video introductions of themselves and a Q&A forum was set up for the students to exchange information about themselves based on the videos. In the second phase, the students studied two local artists—one from Catalonia and one from Ontario—and then exchanged information about their chosen artists online in pairs. This information was used by one of the researchers to build an art gallery in Second Life that included paintings by the two artists. Then the classes visited the art gallery as a group via an **avatar**, a cartoon-like figure which can move around the 3D environment of Second Life and can interact via text and voice with other avatars. In the third and final phase, the students created an e-book together based on the idea that the artists had become friends, describing adventures they had together inspired by the paintings the students had viewed in the virtual gallery. The researchers provided a detailed analysis of the second phase of the project—in the art gallery in Second Life—with the Catalan six-year-old EFL students. This phase took place over several class periods—six language periods in three weeks—and included activities such as the students giving directions to the avatar to explore the art gallery and listening to descriptions of paintings written by their Canadian exchange partners in order to find these paintings in the virtual gallery. Data were collected via video and audio recordings of all the classes, as was other output from the students, teacher and student feedback, and data from post-project recall activities. The researchers found that the students did indeed develop across all competences; in addition, they pointed out that the project design provided opportunities for the students to experience the 'Five Cs' described by the American Council on Teaching of Foreign Languages as key for supporting effective language learning: *communication, cultures, connections, comparisons,* and *communities.* According to the researchers, the students experienced *communication* by practicing oral production of the foreign language—English for the Catalan students; they experienced *cultures* by learning about art in two different countries; they experienced *connections* through cross-curricular tasks, for example art, geography, map reading, and technology; they experienced *comparisons* by developing insights into how language can be used online; and finally, they experienced *communities* by being safely introduced into a multicultural, multilingual online 3D environment and community, Second Life. ■

Although the use of public collaborative online spaces with children is not widespread, there are also examples of primary school educators using social networking tools such as Twitter (for example, Ziemke, 2012) and Facebook (for example, at Kent Elementary School in Canada). Parents are usually consulted and involved in these kinds of initiatives, which have as their main aim to connect the primary classroom with the world beyond, including with parents.

There are also educators using age-appropriate online games or virtual worlds with primary-level EFL students (for example, Mawer & Stanley, 2011). A large-scale study carried out by Suh, Kim, and Kim (2010) with 220 elementary school EFL students in South Korea examined the effects of taking part in a **MMORPG (Massively Multiplayer Online Role-Playing Game)** on language learning. Participants in the experimental group took part in team-based gameplay during two 40-minute classes a week, over a period of two months. Results showed that students in the experimental group achieved higher scores in post-treatment listening, reading, and writing tests compared to students in the control group who underwent traditional classroom instruction. In addition, the researchers found that students' prior knowledge affected their motivation and performance in the game, as did technical issues with computer bandwidth. Despite the positive findings, Peterson (2012) points out that the researchers did not report on the learners' in-game interactions or language output, nor were learner attitudes to the game explored.

Taking part in MMORPGs is generally considered to be more suited to secondary school students and young adults, and we will examine more research into the potential of these online spaces to support language learning in Chapter 4.

Activity 3.3

Look at the notes you made in response to the questions in Activity 3.1. Now that you have read about research into learning technologies with young learners, can you answer these questions more fully? Can you support your answers by drawing on the research? Have any of your answers changed? Do you feel that some of the questions cannot be answered on the basis of what you have read? Can you suggest how answers to those questions might be found through research?

Summary

Any learning technologies used in the primary classroom need to be aligned to the children's various stages of development. In addition, deployment of technology with primary school students needs to address issues such as screen time and e-safety so that it is used in a beneficial way. Large-scale programs, such as the One Laptop Per Child (OLPC) initiative with XO laptops, or one-to-one initiatives carried out with other hardware such as netbooks or tablets have produced mixed results. These programs tend to fail when a techno-centric view is taken—that is, when the hardware itself is seen as the solution to learning. They tend to produce more positive results when a wider ecological view is taken—that is, when the hardware is seen as just one of a wide range of factors influencing learning, such as the design of appropriate curricula and learning materials, access to technological infrastructure and support, and effective teacher training, and a staged and regularly evaluated rollout is undertaken.

Classroom-based research into how learning technologies might support the development of primary school students' English language reading, writing, speaking, or listening skills, or the development of their intercultural competence, also shows mixed results. Differences in the design and methodology of research mean that it is difficult to make direct comparisons between studies and across contexts; nevertheless, in some contexts and with some technologies positive outcomes can be identified. In these cases, though, it is not always the hardware or software itself that drives the learning; rather, what seems to be key is the role of learning technologies in supporting student motivation and allowing for enhanced learning opportunities—for example, the opportunity to communicate in real time with children in other parts of the world, as in Spotlight Study 3.3.

The mixed research results that we have seen in this chapter with young learners are mirrored in Chapter 4, where we look in detail at research into technologies deployed in the support of second or foreign English language learning with adolescent learners.

4

Learning Technologies Research and Adolescent Learners

Preview

In this chapter, we turn our attention to research into the impact of learning technologies in secondary school classrooms. In North America, this corresponds to middle and high school students, aged from approximately 13 to 18 years old. As in previous chapters, we first identify a number of wider issues that are relevant to technology and adolescents. These are important because they form the backdrop to any attempted use of technology in the secondary school classroom. First, we look at how teenagers use technologies in school and how their use of personal technologies affects issues such as online identity and behavior; all of this impacts teachers both directly and indirectly. We also examine language online and consider how digital media has given rise to new genres, particularly in writing. We end the first part of the chapter with a consideration of the rise of blended learning, particularly in K–12 North American contexts, and what this technology-supported approach means for second language learning. In the second part of the chapter, we review studies that focus on the potential role of technology in vocabulary acquisition, as well as in the development of the four skills: reading, writing, speaking, and listening.

Teenagers and Technology

Like young learners, adolescents have very differing needs and characteristics depending on their ages; they, too, are at different stages of development. Nevertheless, by the time they reach secondary school, students' cognitive reasoning abilities and motor skills are more developed than those of children at primary school. In addition, teenagers often have far greater access to technology than younger children. For example, by 2015, 87 percent of 13- to 17-year-olds in the USA had access to a cell phone (Lenhart, 2015). In North America, teenagers can spend significant amounts of time using technology, both inside and outside school. In Chapter 2, we examined some of the out-of-school uses of technology by North American teenagers; below we look at how they use technology at school.

Technology at School

Even in schools where the use of personal devices is prohibited, adolescent students often find ways to use their devices during class time. Peck et al. (2015) investigated how young people in two US high schools—one urban and one suburban—interacted with technology at school. The study took an ethnographic approach, gathering qualitative data via student interviews, on-site observations, and document analysis. It examined how students took part in school-sanctioned, instructor-led technology activities—such as using school computers to carry out quiz-style multiple-choice exercises or viewing class content on the interactive whiteboard—as well as taking part in more traditional lecture-style or discussion classes with no technology. At the same time, the study also observed how these students found ways to use their own mobile technologies during the school day, despite bans on the use of these technologies at both schools.

In this study, wider issues like excessive screen time (see Chapter 3) or the importance of friendship-driven technology practices for teenagers (see Chapter 2) were also played out in educational contexts. The researchers suggest that teachers need to understand the multifaceted and complex digital practices their adolescent students engage in. They also point out that decades-old teacher-centered instructional practices continue to be the norm, even when school-sanctioned technologies are used by teachers—and students. In addition, they echo the view of many researchers we have mentioned in previous chapters that educational technology is not a magic bullet: by itself, it does not lead to improved learning outcomes.

Online Identity and Online Behaviors

For many teenagers, the internet is not just another tool. It is an online space in which friendships are forged and maintained—and sometimes lost. As sociologist danah boyd explains, over the last decade or more, public spaces have become less accessible to teenagers, and parents increasingly keep children and teenagers at home or occupied with extracurricular activities after school. Faced with few opportunities to interact in non-structured environments with peers, online spaces become one of the few arenas in which teenagers are able to socialize without adult supervision. Today's teenagers learn how to negotiate their social relationships online. Teenagers are also in the process of forming their own identities, and much of this takes place online. Social networking sites and other online environments provide teenagers with arenas in which to work out who they are and who they want to be (boyd, 2014).

Digital literacies curricula for secondary school students frequently include a focus on online behavior, such as how to protect one's privacy on social networking sites, how to avoid cyberbullying, and other general e-safety issues. Although some of these issues are also relevant to primary school students, the focus with secondary school learners is different. Adolescent students are usually more autonomous with technology than younger learners; indeed, parents often have limited control over their teenagers' digital lives. Teenagers may also use online spaces to navigate complex issues such as sexual identity, which can result in inappropriate online behavior like **sexting**. This is a widespread global phenomenon (Chalfen, 2009); surveys in the USA suggest that one in five teenagers have shared inappropriate images of themselves with others (Gillespie, 2011), despite the practice being a felony in many countries. Schubert and Wurf (2014) examined a wide range of ICT school policies and curricula documents pertaining to sexting at lower secondary schools in Australia. They found that teachers are automatically assumed to be proficient in digital skills *and* in legislation pertaining to illegal practices such as sexting. The researchers argued that this unfairly puts teachers at legal risk and that teachers need to be trained in 'legal literacy' to be able to successfully deal with the more serious safety issues that can affect adolescents.

Language Online

Teenage behavior is not the only thing that is influenced by communicating online; language itself has undergone changes with the rise of digital media. Sociologists point to the increasing **informalization** of relationships in modern times, a trend which has increased with online communication and is reflected in language used online in digital media. Teachers, for example, are often concerned about young learners' use of overly casual language and so-called 'text speak' in writing, where short forms such as 'u' instead of 'you' are commonplace. There is a concern that genres like text speak are eroding literacy standards; however, this is a view that has been thoroughly refuted (for example, Baron, 2008; Crystal, 2011). For instance, Plester and Wood (2009) found a positive correlation between the ability to use text speak and standard spelling conventions at school among British preteens.

It is undeniable that digital communication has given rise to new genres or 'technolects' (Simpson & Walker, 2014): what Crystal (2006) refers to as 'netspeak' or, more recently, as 'outputs' (2011). There is no doubt that the language used in a tweet is different from that used in a Facebook status update, which is in turn different from that used in an email. Nevertheless, according to Crystal (2011), changes to language brought about by digital communication take place primarily at the level of vocabulary—with the emergence of new words—and orthography—with new abbreviations, the use of emoticons, etc. Least change is seen at the level of syntax and grammar. Because many online spaces for communication are new, so new language forms and conventions are continually emerging, although these are frequently ignored in formal education. For example, the rise of mobile computing has led to 'additional change in the ways that we communicate, such as blurring the boundaries between email, SMS, and social network messages' (Walker & White, 2013, p. 26). Given this shifting linguistic landscape, Walker and White (2013) suggest that rather than trying to teach students different 'genres' of writing, for example, email or SMS, it is more effective for teachers to identify the context and features of a specific online communicative event and help students use the language that is appropriate to that event. In other words, teachers should focus on helping students with the language they need to take part in real online communication with others. This reflects a view of literacy as social practices rather than as a static set of skills, and fits well with Gillen's conception of digital literacies that we explored in Chapter 2.

In terms of research into language online, there have been four main approaches to date (Barton & Lee, 2013). First of all, there are studies that focus on the structural features of online language, for example the use of emoticons, netspeak, or online language corpora. Secondly, there are studies that focus on how language is used online in a variety of social contexts, for example in blogs or in SMS messages. This approach considers how gender, cultural, and linguistic differences are revealed in language choices; it also includes soliciting users' perceptions of their own online language use. Thirdly, there are studies that focus on how *language ideologies* and *metalanguage* are reflected in online utterances. This approach examines how online communication can be shaped by social ideologies—what one believes about language—and metalinguistic discourse—the language used to talk about language. For example, native speakers communicating via text chat with language learners online may display concern over the learners' use of text speak instead of standard linguistic forms, reflecting social ideologies of fear of a decline in standards, possibly gleaned from debates in the mass media. As another example, native speakers communicating with non-native speakers online may use self-deprecating metalanguage to downplay their own linguistic abilities. Groups of non-native speakers communicating online may discuss translation issues or nuances of L2 meaning in a certain phrase, displaying metalinguistic awareness. Finally, a more recent approach to analyzing online language is by framing studies within concepts like **superdiversity** and **supermobility**—both products of our increasingly globalized world.

Learning Online

Over the past decade, there has been a significant increase in the number of K–12 students learning online in all subject areas—including core subjects like English language arts and math—particularly in North America. Some predict that 50 percent of all high school courses will be delivered online by 2019 (Christensen, Horn, & Johnson, 2008). In Canada, approximately five percent of all K–12 students studied online in 2014, and this number is rising (Barbour, 2014); in some provinces, Canada has the highest per capita student enrolment in online courses and programs in the world (Canuel, 2013). Canada, like Australia, has long been a pioneer in distance learning due to its vast geography; nevertheless, although access has traditionally been a driver for distance learning in Canada, online learning in K–12 has more recently emerged as a cost-effective alternative to traditional face-to-face education (Canuel, 2013).

In the USA, particularly, learning online has seen significant growth. Individual schools—for example, Carpe Diem Collegiate High School or Rocketship Education elementary schools—and entire school districts—such as Florida Virtual School—offer part of their curriculum online, in what is known as a blended, or hybrid, learning mode. In blended mode, students study part of the curriculum independently at home—possibly with online tutors for additional support and guidance—or inside the school building in computer labs, where tutors are available to guide and help students as necessary. The percentage of online work versus face-to-face classroom work varies widely. Classroom Snapshot 4.1 from the Carpe Diem school describes how one such blended model works in practice.

Classroom Snapshot 4.1

A large room filled with 280 cubicles with computers—similar in layout to a call center—sits in the middle of Carpe Diem's current building. Students rotate every 55 minutes between self-paced online learning in this large learning center and face-to-face instruction in traditional classrooms. When students are learning online in the learning center, paraprofessionals offer instant direction and help as students encounter difficulties. In the traditional classroom, a teacher re-teaches, enhances, and applies the material introduced online. Students attend class four days a week, although the days are longer (7:30 a.m. to 4 p.m.). Only students who need extra assistance come to the school on Friday. […]

In the Carpe Diem learning center, if a student struggles for more than three minutes with the concept, the e2020 system (e2020 is the online-learning content provider) alerts an assistant coach, who responds with immediate, on-the-spot help. This simple alert motivates students to stay on task and helps resolve problems quickly. Rather than slapping a failing grade on a report card at the end of the course, Carpe Diem's system helps students experience repeated, frequent successes. Carpe Diem works each day with students to make sure that they master each small increment of learning. Just as in a video game, students do not move on to the next level or unit until they have passed. As students move through each task, the software displays their progress in a bar along the top of the webpage. The progress bar moves from red, to yellow, to green, and then to blue if they are ahead of pace. The software provides continual feedback, assessment, and incremental victory in a way that a face-to-face teacher with a class of 30 students never could. After each win, students continue to move forward at their own pace.

(Horn & Staker, 2011) ▇

Drivers for blended learning include a shortage of teachers for classroom instruction, a lack of space, and reduced school budgets, as well as the belief that blended learning may lead to improved results on standardized tests (Horn & Staker, 2011). The spread of blended learning at K–12 has both supporters and detractors. Supporters cite a more personalized approach to learning that allows students to work at their own pace with curricular content that is adapted to their level, as well as the need for fewer specialized teachers and the ability of teachers to use classroom time more productively on high-value activities like critical thinking and project-based learning. Detractors, on the other hand, question the value of so-called personalized learning delivered by computers that essentially present students with the same pre-packaged content (for example, Watters, 2015; Enyedy, 2014). In addition, detractors question the widespread deployment of educational technology hardware and software in schools, despite a lack of research into its effectiveness (Cuban, 2015d).

Some early research into the effectiveness of blended learning in K–12 make a case for cautious optimism. One example comes from a 2014 study of almost 5,000 K–12 students attending 23 US public charter schools implementing blended learning practices. On the basis of data generated over a period of two years, the researchers found that students made significantly greater gains in math and reading compared to students in schools with no blended approaches (Rand Corporation, 2014). Nevertheless, the report also included the caveat that:

> it is not yet possible to identify which particular instructional approaches may account for the positive student learning outcomes identified in math and reading.
>
> (Rand Corporation, 2014, p. 5)

When looking at students' scores on standardized tests in Rocketship Education elementary schools, which have a similar approach to Carpe Diem, Lafer (2014) reports that over a longer term there is a significant drop in student achievement while using technology.

Looking more closely at how effectively blended programs might support foreign language learning, the picture is unclear. For example, not all US schools are required to report either student achievement data or language proficiency benchmark data, so it is difficult to draw conclusions about students' achievement in a blended approach. In addition, there is wide variation in the amount of time students spend on supplemental online courses—that is, additional online courses that take place outside of school hours. Formative assessment may not take place at all, which means that teachers are unaware of students' progress until a final summative assessment at the end of a semester or school year (Lin & Warschauer, 2015). These researchers also point out that to succeed in unsupported online learning, students need a high capacity for self-regulation, which is impacted by learner motivation, and this is not necessarily a trait of low-achieving students. A study of North Carolina Virtual Public School (Oliver, Kellogg, & Patel, 2012) found that high school students taking online foreign language courses had significantly less favorable opinions of their courses than students studying other subjects online. In addition, only 19 percent of intermediate and advanced foreign language students felt that they learned as much in their online courses as in offline courses. Despite the lack of research, blended learning in K–12 is a trend that shows no sign of slowing down in the coming years. Clearly, there is an urgent need for research into its effectiveness on language learning outcomes and achievement in both primary and secondary school contexts.

Learning Technologies Research with Secondary School Learners

In this section, we review a number of studies that focus on the role that technology may play in supporting second language learning for secondary school learners. Some of the studies focus on a single language area or skill—for example, vocabulary or reading—while others focus on two or more skills; some of the studies are classroom-based while others take place in informal out-of-class online settings; some of the studies are 'learning-outcomes-oriented' while others are 'learning-opportunities-oriented' (Ware & Hellmich, 2014; see also Chapter 3). We start with one of the most frequently researched areas: the effect of multimedia on vocabulary acquisition and reading comprehension. We then look at studies focusing on the four skills—reading, writing, listening, and speaking—followed by research into the online spaces that teenagers inhabit, both in formal classroom settings and 'in the wild' (Thorne, 2009)—that is, in informal, out-of-class contexts.

Research into Vocabulary Acquisition and the Effect of Multimedia

As we saw in Chapter 1, during the 1990s, personal computer capabilities developed to include multimedia: graphics, sound, and later, video; this enabled the development of CD-ROM multimedia language learning materials. Multimedia and, specifically, the effect of multimodal learning—that is, learning through different combinations of sight and/or sound—has been a focus of learning technologies researchers for decades. Most early research into the effect of multimedia learning materials on the acquisition of vocabulary and improvements in reading comprehension with English language learners took place in university contexts (see Chun & Plass, 1996, 1997, for an overview). In contrast, in K–12 contexts in the USA, early research focused more generally on the effect of multimedia on the development of L1 literacy. Nevertheless, computers became increasingly available in both ESL and EFL contexts, and by 2010, research into the effect of multimedia on primary and secondary school English language learners had begun to emerge.

For language learners, it has been suggested that processing new information in many modes at the same time can lead to excessive **cognitive load** (Sweller, 2005). In other words, if language learners, especially at lower levels of proficiency, need to process text, visuals, and audio/video information simultaneously, this may overload their working memory and they may be unable to integrate these multiple sources of information, which can lead to a breakdown in comprehension (Abraham, 2008). Research in ESL and EFL contexts seems to both support and contradict these claims.

Silverman and Hines (2009) carried out a study with pre-kindergarten, kindergarten, first-grade, and second-grade students in the USA and found gains in vocabulary acquisition via shared readings supported with multimedia, as opposed to traditional print-based shared readings. This research concluded that the judicious use of multimedia can support vocabulary acquisition and reading comprehension for ELLs—that is, when the information is presented in multiple modes simultaneously, for example text, visuals, and/or audio/video. Another US-based study investigated the effects of a multimedia web-based program called ESL ReadingSmart on reading comprehension with 66 Hispanic secondary school ELLs, with students using the program for 45 minutes, three times a week, over a period of eight months (Cuellar, de la Colina, Episcopo, Hollier, & Leavell, 2009). The researchers found significant improvements in the ELLs' reading scores after the treatment, suggesting that the multimedia approach helped students develop their reading comprehension skills over a period of time.

However, different findings were reported in an EFL context by Lin and Yu (2012). Thirty-two junior high school students in Taiwan used a cell phone **MMS**-based vocabulary learning program during a period of four weeks. The program delivered nine new vocabulary words a week to the students via the cell phones in one of four modes:

1   via text only—a word, its syntactic category, the Chinese translation, and an example sentence
2   via text + audio—including pronunciation of the new word/sentence
3   via text + image—including an image representing the meaning of the word
4   via text + audio + image—that is, via all three modes simultaneously.

Students evaluated the program very positively, but in post-tests, no significant difference was found between the effects of the different presentation modes on vocabulary acquisition. In other words, in this study a single mode—text, with a Chinese translation—was found to be as effective for acquisition as providing the new vocabulary with multimedia support.

Nevertheless, another Taiwanese study did find differences in vocabulary acquisition depending on the mode of delivery. A study with seventh-grade EFL learners carried out by Lin and Tseng (2012) examined the effects of animated illustrations or videos on the acquisition of what were considered complex—that is, difficult to define—vocabulary words. This study compared the effects of three modes—text only, text and graphics, and text and videos—on vocabulary acquisition, which was measured via both immediate and delayed post-tests. Of the three modes, the researchers found that video support was most effective in helping students retain the target vocabulary and suggested that video annotations should be more widely used by teachers to help their students learn challenging vocabulary.

Another area that interests researchers is how captions with multimedia might support EFL students' vocabulary acquisition, as described in Spotlight Study 4.1.

Spotlight Study 4.1

A study with 32 13- to 14-year-old junior high school Chinese EFL students carried out by Lwo and Chia-Tzu Lin (2012) examined the use of captions to support learning in computer-animated vocabulary lessons based on two scientific articles. The students were divided into four groups based on their proficiency in English, and four caption types were investigated with each group: no captions, Chinese captions, English captions, and Chinese plus English captions. Post-tests and semi-structured interviews showed that the effect of captions depended on the students' L2 proficiency. Lower-proficiency students performed better with English and with Chinese plus English captions relative to students with no captions. The researchers suggested that lower-proficiency students 'relied on graphics and animation as an important tool for understanding English sentences'

(Lwo & Chia-Tzu Lin, 2012, p. 188). ▦

Studies with university students mirror the mixed results above, with some studies showing a positive effect for certain combinations of multimedia and other studies showing positive effects for the opposite combinations. Not only are the results for university-age young adults mixed, but in some cases, it has been found that multimedia glosses do not aid comprehension significantly (Ariew & Ercetin, 2004); others have found a negative correlation between reading comprehension and the use of pronunciation, audio, and video annotations (Sakar & Ercetin, 2005). Reviewing the studies in this chapter, one can conclude that additional factors may have influenced whether or not multimedia supported vocabulary acquisition but that these factors were not examined in the studies—for example, ESL versus EFL contexts; whether translation was provided; the educational culture of the students, such as whether rote memorization is a favored study technique; the age and language proficiency level of the students;

the different instructional approaches and task design; the complexity of the new vocabulary; the length of the study, etc. What is clear is that it is extremely difficult to make sweeping statements about what supports or does not support language acquisition when we attempt to isolate and focus purely on the role of technology—multimedia in this case.

Vocabulary and Cell Phones: SMS

The increasing ubiquity of mobile devices—especially cell phones—has opened up new avenues of research in the field of vocabulary acquisition. Researchers have been especially interested in the unique ability of the cell phone to send short chunks of content—such as vocabulary words or short sentences—to students via SMS, as well as in the cell phone's potential for delivering content based on a student's geographical location via its GPS tracking function.

A study in Taiwan by Lu (2008) investigated the effectiveness of SMS messages on 30 EFL high school students' vocabulary acquisition. In one week, 15 students—half of the group—received a printed list of 14 target English/Chinese word pairs; the other half of the group received two target word pairs a day via SMS message. The following week, the two groups swapped the way they received a second set of 14 word pairs. Vocabulary tests administered at the end of each week showed vocabulary acquisition gains for the students in both groups; in addition, no significant differences were found in further post-treatment testing three weeks later. This study therefore suggests that the delivery mode of the vocabulary—SMS messages versus paper—made no difference to vocabulary acquisition.

An Iranian study, also carried out with 30 EFL high school students, found very different results (Tabatabaei & Goojani, 2012). During a two-month period, the students received five or six words per class via SMS and wrote a sentence including each word to illustrate its meaning. A control group of 30 students carried out the same activity but received words written on paper. The SMS group significantly outperformed the control group on a vocabulary post-test; in addition, the experimental group and their teachers displayed positive attitudes towards the SMS approach to vocabulary learning.

Location-based vocabulary learning supported by mobile devices is another area that has been explored by researchers. Chen and Li (2010) described the design and prototype testing with EFL students of a context-aware vocabulary learning system called PCULS (Personalized Context-aware Ubiquitous Learning System). Via GPS tracking, or **geotagging**, mobile devices delivered English/Chinese word pairs to students based on their location; the reasoning behind this was that context-specific vocabulary related to real-life situations would be far more meaningful and memorable for students. The system was trialed with 36 tenth-grade students at 12 different locations in a high school in Taiwan. Over a period of two weeks, half of the students—the experimental group—studied the English/Chinese word pairs via PCULS; the other half of the students— the control group—studied the same word pairs without the technology. In post-treatment vocabulary tests, 94 percent of the experimental group showed gains in vocabulary learning compared to 67 percent of the control group. In addition, 72 percent of the experimental group expressed a preference for context-aware vocabulary learning support.

Activity 4.1

The mixed results found in the three SMS studies described above illustrate some of the caveats in research studies that we outlined in Chapter 3 and make it difficult to generalize about learning outcomes. For example, the studies take place over short time frames; they involve small groups of students; and they do not consider the importance of external factors, such as learners' ages, interests, proficiency levels, previous knowledge, and levels of motivation.

Choose one of the studies above and consider how you could redesign it to make it more robust. Apart from taking into account the caveats, consider also what theoretical perspective you would take (see Chapter 2) and consider whether you might collect qualitative and/or quantitative data.

Perhaps what this section on learning technologies and vocabulary acquisition via SMS illustrates is that learning is best understood as a cultural practice arising from the complex interplay between actors—both students and teachers—tools, and sociocultural/sociohistorical contexts. It lends support to Hubbard's observation that the role of technology in language learning is 'most properly viewed not as computers teaching people, but as people teaching people through the medium of computers' (1996, p. 32).

Vocabulary and Cell Phones: Geotagging

Geotagging has the potential to deliver multimedia content, not only vocabulary, to students based on their geographical location; some studies have explored the impact of this on informal out-of-class learning. We discussed a study incorporating this approach in Chapter 3 with elementary students in the Netherlands (see page 82). The European-Union-funded

MASELTOV project in the UK and Europe, and the Mentira project in the USA, have both developed this concept with adult language learners, with promising results. The MASELTOV project (a partial acronym for Mobile Assistance for Social Inclusion and Empowerment of Immigrants with Persuasive Learning Technologies and Social Network Services) is aimed at migrants living in the UK, Germany, and Spain who need to learn local languages to more fully participate in the societies to which they have migrated. Language assistance is provided to these learners on mobile devices, via automated language tasks as well as a context-aware recommender system, which provides users with relevant language or information depending on their geographical location. For example, if the user is at a train station, the system, installed on the user's mobile device, suggests useful language for buying a ticket or for enquiring about train times; if the user is visiting a medical center, key expressions to use with a doctor are suggested. These expressions convey not just key vocabulary but also **pragmatic meaning**. Users can use social networking features built into the system to communicate directly with real volunteers nearby, who can support them linguistically in these contexts if needed.

The Mentira project is aimed at university students of Spanish—*mentira* means 'lie' in Spanish; it uses an **augmented reality** murder mystery game interface to provide learners with clues delivered via their smart mobile devices while they visit a Spanish-speaking neighborhood in Albuquerque, New Mexico, USA. Students follow in-game instructions to find key places in the neighborhood, and they sometimes need to interact with the local residents in Spanish as they seek further information to solve the murder mystery (see Pegrum, 2014, for a detailed description of these projects). They offer an interesting possible avenue of exploration for providing context-specific linguistic content and motivating activities to adolescents who have access to smartphones—something which, as we have noted, is becoming increasingly common in many contexts.

Research into Reading Comprehension

Researchers tend to agree that the internet provides a rich source of authentic reading materials for language learners and that this is, overall, a positive thing (for example, Levine, Ferenz, & Reves, 2000; Brandl, 2002; Gambrell, 2005). The internet includes traditional texts, such as newspaper and magazine articles or academic papers, in electronic format, but it has also enabled the creation of digital text which can be read in new ways. Online texts often have hyperlinks which lead to other web pages; they can include images and other multimedia; they can be created by anyone with a device and internet connection; they can have multiple authors and readers; and readers can interact with writers, for example via blog comments. Some forms of online text, such as **interactive fiction**, require the reader to make choices as they read, and their choices affect the plot of a story. By installing **plug-ins**, the reader can translate entire online texts into other languages at the press of a button; the translation of individual words or glosses in the same language can appear when the cursor is held over a word in an online text. In sum, reading is no longer a solitary, linear process but can now involve interactivity with the text, and collaboration with other readers and writers. What does this mean for research into reading in a second or foreign language?

One area that has particularly interested researchers is whether reading online texts—or hypertext—rather than paper texts can help or hinder reading comprehension. For example, Lück (2008) investigated the effects of pedagogically guided web-based reading on the development of skimming and scanning skills and on motivation and participation with a group of 46 high school students learning German as a foreign language in the USA, over the course of a semester. The students were in two separate classes: one class formed the experimental group while the other class formed the control group. Both groups read texts about German politics and culture, with the experimental group reading hypertext online and the control group reading traditional linear paper-based texts. The study found that although both groups increased their skimming and scanning reading skills, the experimental group significantly outperformed the control group, and those who had read hypertexts during the experiment were also able to deploy their skimming and scanning skills with paper-based texts. In addition, the experimental group showed significant gains in motivation and participation. The researcher suggested that the results of this study indicated that traditional reading texts in the foreign language classroom should be supplemented with guided web-based reading so as to provide students with a variety of reading approaches.

The medium—for example, online versus paper-based texts—is not the only area that has interested researchers. With the rise of mobile computing, the devices used to deliver reading texts have also come under scrutiny. For instance, researchers have examined whether students prefer to read texts on electronic devices, via email, or on paper.

Activity 4.2

A study carried out in Taiwan with ten 12th-grade EFL high school students examined three different devices or modes for the delivery of reading texts (Huang & Lin, 2011). The study explored students' preferences for reading shorter or longer English language texts on cell phones compared to on paper or via email. The study proposed the following research questions:

1   Do learners prefer reading shorter texts on mobile phones to reading them on other media? Do learners have different preferences when reading longer texts?

2   What advantages and disadvantages can learners perceive when reading shorter texts on mobile phones, via email, and on paper? Do learners have different perceptions of advantages and disadvantages when reading longer texts?

(Huang & Lin, 2011, p. 62)

The students received two sets of narrative text: one set of three longer texts of 786–898 words each, and one set of three shorter texts of 54–60 words each. Each set of three texts was delivered on paper, via email, and via cell phone; students could read the texts at their own pace at any time. Quantitative data on students' attitudes were collected via questionnaires after they had finished reading each set of texts. The students also wrote a summary of each text in the questionnaire so that the researchers could gauge their understanding.

What do you think the researchers found in response to their research questions? Do you think these secondary school students had a preference for the mode of delivery of the texts?

Huang and Lin found that the majority of students preferred the paper format for both sets of texts, although the difference in preferences was not significant. For the shorter texts, students preferred the cell phone over email. For the longer texts, the cell phone was the least preferred delivery device, mainly because of the small screen size and font. Although the researchers cautioned against generalizing about students' preferred delivery mode for texts because of the very small sample size in this study, they suggested that students' preferences may be a fruitful area for future research.

Finally, the extent to which access to immediate translation can affect reading comprehension is another area of interest to researchers. In an ethnographic study carried out in Canada, Li (2009) investigated 24 Chinese-speaking ESL high school students' use of vocabulary learning strategies while reading technology-enhanced texts, as opposed to reading texts with no technology support. The technology support consisted of providing the ELLs with immediate translations of English words they did not understand, in Chinese, so as to instantly increase their word comprehension ability—a key skill in reading comprehension. The study found that the students reading technology-supported texts used a significantly wider variety of strategies compared to the students who had no access to the technology.

Research into Writing

With Web 2.0, it has become increasingly easy for anyone to produce text online. Students can create individual written blogs or take part in class blogs; they can contribute to class-based wikis or public wikis like Wikipedia; they can produce short snippets of writing on social networking sites such as Twitter and Facebook. As we saw earlier in this chapter (see page 97), these new genres of digital text begin to blur the boundaries between writing and speaking. It has been suggested that online reading and writing is strongly influencing general literacy practices and written culture, and that the ease with which anyone can publish or access digital texts is resulting in what Baron (2008) calls 'snippet literacy'. Baron describes this as her university students' desire to read only short pieces of text rather than whole books, and their tendency to use online search functions to engage only with very short extracts online rather than with extended texts. These arguments may be true to a certain extent; on the other hand, the ease with which language learners are now able to create digital text means that they can potentially read and write online—in a foreign or second language—for a wide audience of readers, and they are also able to interact and communicate with real communities of readers and writers.

For this and other reasons we explore below, writing is a skill that has received a substantial amount of attention in learning technologies research, primarily in university contexts but also at secondary school level. Two main research areas have emerged (Ware & Hellmich, 2014): the use of software to automatically evaluate students' writing and a focus on writing processes enabled by socially oriented Web 2.0 tools—for example, writing on wikis, blogs, online forums, and social networking sites. We examine these two research areas in the sections below.

Automated Writing Evaluation

Automated writing evaluation (AWE) software, also known as 'Automated Essay Scoring' (AES) software, compares students' written work with large corpora of writing and analyzes measurable features such as syntax, discourse features, and vocabulary range through statistical modelling and algorithms. A student's essay is given an overall score as well as editorial suggestions for improvements at the word level, and feedback comments are included on the student's overall writing style; this latter feedback is standardized so that all students who receive a certain score on a certain genre of essay will get exactly the same feedback comments.

There are criticisms of AWE, such as the software's inability to judge critical thinking, rhetorical knowledge, creativity, or a student's ability to tailor texts to a specific readership; in other words, much criticism revolves around AWE software's inability to evaluate writing as a socially embedded process, with all the nuances that this entails.

Nevertheless, AWE programs have been deployed in secondary, middle, and elementary school classrooms, and some positive impacts have been identified. For example, the use of AWE software has been found to encourage students to review their written work (Chapelle, 2008; Warschauer & Grimes, 2008). A study into the effect of AWE used by language arts teachers in US secondary schools found that students' motivation for writing increased (Warschauer & Grimes, 2008). However, when the researchers analyzed their findings in more detail, they identified three paradoxes: firstly, although students and teachers reported positive attitudes towards AWE, they criticized the accuracy of its scoring and feedback; secondly, despite students' positive attitudes, they did not write more frequently; and thirdly, there was no time scheduled for students to review and revise their essays during class in the light of AWE feedback, despite a desire to do so.

In a multi-site, longitudinal analysis of AWE programs in several middle schools, Grimes and Warschauer (2010) found that students were motivated to write by the programs, which made classroom management easier for teachers. On the other hand, they identified a need for students and teachers to critically evaluate the feedback and scores generated by AWE programs, as well as the need for teachers to deploy these programs in pedagogically sound ways so as to include a range of writing genres and activities for students.

According to Warschauer (2011), interviews with elementary school teachers revealed varied attitudes as to the effectiveness of AWE software;

those teachers with a high percentage of ELLs in their classes preferred to take advantage of Web 2.0 tools that allowed their students to write for authentic audiences; in addition, these elementary teachers' enthusiasm for AWE programs decreased over time. (For a comprehensive overview of research into AWE, see Elliot et al., 2013; for a description of several AWE programs in use in US schools, see Jang, 2014, in this series.)

Activity 4.3

Based on your reading of this section, create a list of the advantages and disadvantages of Automated Writing Evaluation (AWE) software. Can you think of any other possible advantages and disadvantages of AWE? You might like to use a table like the one below.

Advantages	Disadvantages

Writing on Wikis

Since the rise of Web 2.0, wikis have been a popular platform for language teachers attempting to develop their students' writing skills. Because wikis are essentially editable web pages, a single page can easily be edited by several different writers; in addition, the history of the edits made by individuals to a wiki page can be tracked and viewed. As such, wikis lend themselves particularly well to collaborative approaches to writing, by providing teachers with a window on the writing process (Kárpáti, 2009) as well as a record of who wrote what and when on the wiki page. What is more, if a wiki is published online, it provides students with a real audience and thus a more authentic reason for writing. We review several wiki studies below.

Mak and Coniam (2008) carried out a wiki-based project with 24 Year 7 secondary school EFL students in Hong Kong. The students worked together in groups of four and used wikis to produce a brochure about the features and facilities of their new school, which they had joined from primary school a few months previously. The wiki writing project was an integral part of their English language homework and took place over a period of two months. The final versions of the students' brochures were printed and distributed to parents. The researchers analyzed the students' contributions to the group wikis at various stages of the project. Initially, they found that students limited themselves to adding text to the brochures. However, as the project continued, the students started to review and revise each other's written contributions, and a more collaborative approach to writing emerged within the groups, with the students both developing new content on the wiki and editing and expanding existing content.

This social aspect of wikis, in which writers can become part of a more collaborative approach to writing over time, is reflected in a study by Lund (2008). In this Norwegian study, a group of 31 17-year-old English language students produced a wiki about their perceptions of the USA, covering a range of student-proposed topics, such as soap operas. Using a sociocultural approach informed by activity theory, the researcher collected data by video-recording the students' use of the wiki over a period of two weeks during class; a post-intervention questionnaire was also administered to the students, and an analysis of the content produced in the wiki was undertaken. Students worked in pairs and Lund found that they initially worked fairly independently on their chosen topics. However, once the initial production of text had taken place, they began to explore and develop each other's writing, showing evidence of collaborative writing practices.

Writing on Blogs

Researchers have also investigated the potential of blogs to support student writing at secondary school. Like wikis, blogs have the potential to reach a wide readership online and can provide students with a real audience for their writing. As such, it has been argued (for example, by Raith, 2009) that blogs are not simply substitutes for students writing on paper but enable new genres of writing and the development of new contexts for communication, which require students to develop new literacies. Often, blogs are perceived as tools that can motivate students to write more and to write better, and several researchers have argued that they should be adopted by English language teachers for this reason (for example, Ducate & Lomicka, 2005; Hendron, 2003; Murray & Hourigan, 2005).

Raith (2009) examined the use of blogs with 29 Grade 9 EFL students in Germany with a fairly low level of English proficiency—A2 on the **Common European Framework of Reference (CEFR)**. The aim of this six-week qualitative study was to investigate the effect of an online audience on the students' writing process. The students created written journals about their reading of a set book in English and were allowed to choose which medium to write in: 19 students chose to use traditional paper and pen journals and wrote for an imagined/abstract audience, while ten students chose to use blogs and wrote for a real online audience. Data were collected by means of pre- and post-treatment questionnaires and post-treatment focused interviews with the students, as well as from the content of the paper journals and the blogs. The researcher found that both groups of students were acutely aware of audience but that the blog writers showed more focus on meaning in their writing and were keen to interact with their audience about their writing.

Raith's study adds to the positive press that blogging for English language students receives, both in secondary and adult contexts. However, there are voices of caution. A study carried out with a group of 27 Belgian 17-year-old EFL students examined the extent to which blogs motivated the students to write more and to write better, as well as whether the quality of their writing and their understanding of the content under discussion actually improved (Sercu, 2013). Over a period of six weeks, students were given a weekly prompt on a range of topics—such as an international political issue, a recent local health campaign, or their post-high-school plans—and were asked to write a blog post with their reactions to the prompt. The data analysis involved both qualitative and quantitative approaches: questionnaires were administered to the students and two software packages were used to analyze the linguistic complexity of their blog posts. Sercu found that the majority of students were motivated by writing for a real audience and by being able to interact and discuss issues via the comments section on the blog posts; the students also wrote more than usual. However, the researcher did not find conclusive data to demonstrate that the students' writing had improved over the course of the project, possibly because of the short duration of the study and the limited amount of written data produced. In addition, Sercu found that the lower-proficiency students found the project less motivating, wrote less, and preferred reading their classmates' blog posts to producing their own. Sercu concluded that 'blogs work for some students, but not for others' (2013, p. 4364). Nevertheless, the post-treatment questionnaires revealed that the majority of the students felt that their writing had improved and that they had become more aware of the areas in their writing that needed work. The detailed analysis carried out in this study provides a useful counterbalance to claims that blogs are always effective in supporting and developing all students' writing skills. These findings are similar to those found in Spotlight Study 4.2.

Spotlight Study 4.2

A study by Ware and Kessler (2014) investigated how US middle school students interacted via blogs with students of the same age in Spain, who attended a bilingual Spanish-English school. Through a case study analysis, the researchers found that the students tended to post information-seeking questions rather than interpretation questions in their online interactions. In addition, they found that the groups that displayed the most successful interactions tended to use linguistic features such as lexical items, modality, and alignment markers to signal engagement with their partners, whereas the less successful groups used fewer of these features and provided less depth in their responses to their partners. The researchers also identified several methodological considerations for teachers planning to integrate intercultural online projects of this nature with secondary school students: overoptimism about what students might realistically achieve; concern over potential technical difficulties and the constraints of the school calendar; the need to assess students' learning and participation for formative purposes; and how to provide a persuasive case for intercultural collaborative projects to become mainstream in the curriculum. ∎

Writing on Online Discussion Forums

The **online discussion forum** is another early Web 2.0 tool that has attracted the interest of teachers and researchers, particularly because of its potential to connect language students with a wider online audience. In secondary schools, intercultural online exchanges between classes via discussion forums have enabled students to interact with other students in different countries, as we saw in example studies in Chapters 1 and 2 (Kramsch & Thorne, 2002; O'Dowd, 2014; Thorne, 2003).

Savignon and Roithmeier (2004) carried out a study with high school students learning German as a foreign language in the USA and a class of high school EFL students in Germany. The researchers analyzed the language produced by these students in their forum postings in discussions on student-nominated topics—such as the American Dream and the death penalty—lasting about three weeks. They found that the students collaborated in their discussions on the topics and posted additional information at points, integrating information from other posts. In addition, the students' writing contained a range of vocabulary and ideas; they used cohesive devices to strengthen their arguments; they cited online research to support their views; and they used effective linguistic strategies to avoid potential conflicts in communication, such as using subject headings in posts, or using questions or comments at the end of a posting to soften the message. For the learners in this particular study, the online forum discussions appeared to develop both their language skills and their communication skills.

Focusing on 29 English language learners in four high schools in the USA, Hill (2010) carried out a mixed-methods study to evaluate the effects of taking part in an asynchronous discussion forum on the ELLs' writing skills. Based on pre- and post-test data from students in the experimental group, who took part in the online forum discussions, and from students in the control group, who did not take part, Hill found no statistically significant difference in the development of writing skills. Nevertheless, she found that the experimental group showed some improvement in their interpersonal communication skills and that they also expressed positive attitudes to the experience, considering it a good way to make new friends.

Writing on Social Networking Sites

Social networking sites provide a relatively new arena for researchers to investigate the development of students' technolects (see page 97), as well as their identities as second or foreign language learners. Social networking sites are popular with students outside the classroom but are often ignored in formal instructional settings. Thorne and Reinhardt (2008) suggest that 'bridging activities' designed around the use of these sites for language learning can provide a much-needed link between the students' out-of-class lives and what happens inside the classroom.

Social networking sites are often considered more appropriate for adults; however, a qualitative study in South Korea examined how three EFL teachers used the **microblogging** service Twitter with their elementary, middle, and high school students during a three-week period (Kim, 2010). The researchers found that all three teachers' interaction patterns with students were noticeably different when using Twitter. In addition, the three teachers were in agreement that Twitter provided an effective platform for writing practice for their students and gave them a valuable opportunity to spontaneously use English to communicate for authentic purposes.

Research into social networking sites carried out with university students have explored the potential of sites like Facebook and Ning for creating supportive learning communities and opportunities for informal learning (see Harrison & Thomas, 2009; Irwin, Ball, Desbrow, & Leveritt, 2012; Mazer, Murphy, & Simonds, 2007; Souleles, 2012; Blattner & Fiori, 2009; Reinhardt & Zander, 2011).

Perhaps unsurprisingly, uptake of public social networking sites like Facebook in secondary schools has remained low. Since their appearance, teachers and learners have grappled with the issues of privacy foregrounded by these platforms, and legislators have considered moves to ban their use in libraries and schools (boyd & Ellison, 2007). Possibly for these reasons, blogs and wikis have remained the tools of choice for working on writing skills in secondary schools.

Writing to Speaking

As we saw earlier in this chapter (see page 97), some genres of digital writing can display 'speech-like characteristics' (Crystal, 2006, p. 32). For example, the language used in SMS text messages and in instant messaging apps often feels closer to spoken than to written language; in text messages, emoticons can represent prosodic features such as intonation and tone; even loudness can be represented, for example, when caps are used in a message to mimic shouting. Because genres like instant messaging reflect many of the features of spoken language, it has been suggested that interacting in these written genres can help students develop their speaking skills. A study by Satar and Özdener (2008) examined how text chat and voice chat activities might affect a group of secondary school students' speaking proficiency, as well as their anxiety when faced with speaking tasks. The study was carried out with a group of 90 low-proficiency EFL students aged 16 to 17 in Turkey, over a period of four weeks. The students were divided into three groups of 30 students each: one experimental group took part in 40- to 45-minute text chat activities in pairs; the second experimental group took part in 40- to 45-minute voice chat activities, also in pairs; and the third group, the control group, took part in neither. Activity types included **jigsaw tasks**, decision-making tasks, **information gap tasks**, and problem-solving tasks. Data were collected via pre- and post-anxiety scales and speaking tests; questionnaires were also administered to the students. The speaking proficiency of both experimental groups increased; nevertheless, there was a decrease in the anxiety levels for the text chat group only, and these students were more confident about the possibility of speaking to a native speaker. The researchers suggested that lower-proficiency EFL students might find it beneficial to start interacting via text chat activities before taking part in speaking activities.

Research into Listening and Speaking

The internet provides a wealth of authentic listening material for language students in both audio format—for example, radio podcasts—and video format—for example, YouTube videos. White (1998) suggests that online listening materials should provide language students with several opportunities: to choose when and how often to listen; to make their own listening texts and tasks; to engage in listening and speaking with others; to become active rather than passive listeners; and to reflect on why and where they have problems in their understanding/listening. Technology also provides a wealth of tools for language students to practice their speaking skills. For example, **voice recognition software** allows them to communicate with online **chatbots** or avatars, or with mobile-device-based **intelligent assistants**, such as Apple's **Siri**; audio- and videoconferencing tools, such as Skype or Adobe Connect, enable them to communicate with others around the world; they can be encouraged to record their responses to audio prompts delivered via mobile devices; and avatars in virtual worlds or gaming environments allow them to take on a new 'persona' and to communicate with others via that persona (see Spotlight Studies 3.3 and 4.3). Clearly, listening and speaking are very closely connected skills and we examine them together in the following section, looking at studies that integrated some of the tools referred to above.

Speaking Skills and Voice Software

Walker and White (2013) suggest several advantages to language students using voice recognition software—also known as speech recognition software—to communicate with chatbot characters online. Students are not under pressure to communicate fluently on the spot but can take their time to compose the language they want to use. In its standardized reply, the chatbot gives the students a model of pronunciation. It also gives them practice in taking part in fixed question/answer routines, and students need to produce language that is pronounced accurately enough for the chatbot's speech recognition software to understand and respond to. Anecdotal accounts by practicing language teachers (for example, Picardo, 2008) point out that teenage foreign language students find communicating with online chatbots less threatening than interacting with a real person. A study carried out with EFL students in China appears to support this view (see Classroom Snapshot 4.2).

Classroom Snapshot 4.2

A group of 14- and 15-year-old EFL students in China are wearing headsets with microphones and are sitting in front of computers, playing a game. In the game, the students need to interact with virtual characters in a number of different settings in specially designed 3D virtual scenarios. The students need to respond orally to questions asked by virtual characters in the game, which uses speech recognition technology to log and understand their utterances. For example, in one scenario, there is a virtual character who asks the student some questions about a train journey in the UK.

Virtual Character: *Where would you like to go?*
Learner: (no response made)
Virtual Character: *Where would you like to go?*
Learner: *Um.*
Virtual Character: *I would like to go to Oxford. Where would you like to go?*

According to the researchers, the scenarios incorporated:

> various levels of instructional support for the learner, both through spoken audio prompts from the virtual characters and also in the form of text help menus within the scenes for cases where the learner is experiencing some difficulties. Additionally, the virtual tutor character offers implicit spoken feedback to the learner when the learner's utterance has been ungrammatical.

For example:

Virtual Character: *Where would you like to go?*
Learner: *I go to Oxford.*
Virtual Character: *I see. You **would like to** go to Oxford.*

Morton, Gunson, & Jack (2012, pp.4–5) ◼

In their initial trial of this software, Morton and Jack (2010) investigated the uptake and response of two separate groups of students: 48 learners of English in China and 28 learners of French in Scotland. The researchers collected qualitative data on the students' attitudes and motivation towards the program via questionnaires and interviews; they also collected quantitative data on the accuracy of the students' speech, via the program. Findings showed that both groups were very engaged by the program. However, the two groups showed different levels of motivation: the group of Chinese EFL students reported increased positive attitudes, whereas the Scottish students learning French reported increased anxiety levels and decreasing positive attitudes during the study. The researchers suggested that this reflected higher levels of intrinsic motivation in the group of Chinese EFL students. A high level of motivation and engagement with the game was also found in the follow-up study (Morton, Gunson, & Jack, 2012), despite limitations in the speech recognition software. For example, word-for-word recognition performance was as low as 62 percent at times, and the system had difficulties recognizing what the students had said.

Assessment of speaking skills traditionally takes place during class time, with the teacher listening to students carrying out speaking tasks individually, in pairs, or in small groups. Like computer games, the audio-recording features of mobile devices have the potential to move assessment of speaking skills out of the classroom. When students can record their audio output and upload it online, teachers can assess this output at any time, which frees up valuable classroom time for instruction. How might this work in practice? Cooney and Keogh (2007) trialed a commercial software program called Learnosity with 60 high school students learning Irish as a second language over a period of five weeks. The aim of the study was:

> to facilitate school-based oral assessment and students' self-assessment, increase students' communicative competence and motivate students to learn Irish with the fun and familiar props of a mobile phone and web-chat.
>
> (Cooney & Keogh, 2007, p. 1)

Students logged into a **voice response system** via the program on cell phones, listened to questions on a range of topics, and recorded their answers, which were uploaded to a server. Teachers were able to access students' oral responses, which were stored online, and either listen to them online or download them as audio files and listen to them offline; the teachers used these recordings to assess and provide feedback on students' speaking skills. Students could also download and listen to audio files with model answers to the questions. As additional support, students took part in monitored text chat sessions on laptops that provided teacher support. In post-treatment questionnaires, 67 percent of the students reported having made progress in speaking Irish as a result of this pilot project.

Communicating in Online Spaces: Game-Based Learning

Whereas voice software such as that described above allows for limited learner oral output and interactivity, there are other online programs that require much more complex and demanding interaction, both written and spoken. MMORPGs are one example: demanding game-based tasks require communication between players via both text and speech. The potential of MMORPGs to provide meaningful contexts for social interaction via dialog, including peer scaffolding, appears to hold particular promise for language development (Thorne, 2008).

Game-based learning (GBL) is a large field, and a thorough examination of it is beyond the scope of this volume; interested readers are referred to Reinders (2012) for an account of current research. However, we will briefly review GBL and language learning with adolescents, keeping in mind that much research in this area to date has been carried out with young adults rather than with adolescents.

The potential for high-quality, specially designed games to support language learning is well documented. Gee (2012), one of the foremost proponents of complex games as tools for learning, suggests that good games can lower the affective filter by creating engagement and situations where learners' fears are bypassed. Gee proposes that good games can create talk and text, both in the game and outside of it, in an interest-driven site where players discuss the game, gameplay, and problem-solving, gaining metacognitive and metalinguistic skills. Games can lead to hours of practice by placing lower-level skills inside larger, more motivating and engaging problems. But the main thing games can do for language learning, in Gee's view, is to 'situate meaning' (2012, p. xiv).

MMORPGs can provide spaces for students to take part in informal and unstructured language learning out of class time, and we explore this further in Spotlight Study 4.3.

Spotlight Study 4.3

A one-year longitudinal study with 80 15- to 16-year-old students in Sweden studying English in Grade 9 investigated the impact of extramural English activities, including the use of computer games, on oral proficiency and vocabulary acquisition (Sundqvist, 2009). The researcher used interviews, a questionnaire, and language diaries to analyze the students' extramural English activities. In the diaries, the students noted down the amount of time they spent on seven extramural activities: reading books, reading newspapers or magazines, watching television, watching films, using the internet, playing computer games, and listening to music. Sundqvist found that there was a significant positive correlation between the amount of time students spent on extramural English and the size of their vocabulary, which was measured via two vocabulary tests. In addition, she found that the activities that required the students to be productive and rely on their language skills—playing computer games, using the internet, and reading—had a greater impact on vocabulary acquisition.

Sundqvist found a significant gender difference in the amount of time spent playing computer games: the boys played for 7.4 hours per week on average, while the girls played for 0.7 hours per week on average. It was found that gaming benefited the boys' English L2 vocabulary acquisition but did not significantly affect that of the girls. The boys favored MMORPGs which exposed them to plenty of interaction in the target language, whereas the girls preferred more passive, single-player computer games such as *The Sims*. The researcher suggested that the boys' preferred type of gaming was theoretically more beneficial for L2 acquisition than that of the girls. ■

In a US-based study with four Chinese-speaking male adolescents, Li, Chiu, and Coady (2014) examined how taking part in the MMORPG *World of Warcraft* helped these ELLs develop a range of second language literacy strategies. The researchers found that the learners' in-game and out-of-game online interactions included information-seeking, strategizing, socializing, and problem-solving in English. Li et al. suggested that these sorts of informal game-based activities and practices showed strong potential in supporting language acquisition for these adolescent learners.

There is a significant body of research into how MMORPGs can support adult English language learners (for example, Thorne, 2008; Peterson, 2012; Lee & Gerber, 2013) as well as adult learners of other languages, such as German (for example, Bryant, 2006), and Spanish (for example, Palmer, 2010). However, despite predictions dating back over a decade that online games are the future of the classroom (for example, Foreman, 2004), research into how these virtual worlds can support adolescent English language learners remains sparse. In addition, when complex MMORPG are brought into the classroom as part of a more structured learning approach, the reaction of adolescent students in not uniformly positive. For instance, in a study with high school history students, Squire (2005) found that although some of the stronger, more confident students—25 percent overall—reacted positively to playing a MMORPG to learn about history, some of the weaker students—also 25 percent overall—reacted less positively. They found the game too complex and challenging, and their failure to play successfully led to frustration. Squire also found that even among students who viewed themselves as gamers, there was considerable rejection when gameplay became a compulsory part of class, leading him to suggest that educational games do not automatically fit well with tightly prescribed traditional curricula. Students who responded well to the gaming experience preferred hands-on activities and learning by doing, and were typically disaffected by more traditional schooling approaches. Nevertheless, not all of the stronger students reacted well to the game. Successful students felt that their more traditional study expertise was not honored in the game-based classroom, and they were not convinced that success in a MMORPG would help them pass college entrance exams or earn a place in higher education. Squire concludes that complex educational games like MMORPGs are unlikely to find widespread uptake in secondary schools because they do not fit the current social organization of schools. In Squire's words: .

> [t]he real challenge is not so much in bringing games—or any technology—into our schools, but rather changing the culture of our schools to be organized around learning instead of the current form of social control.

(Squire, 2005, pp. 7–8)

Summary

Out of school, adolescents have different access to technologies than primary school students, they use technology more, and they use technologies in a wider variety of ways. Research into the use of learning technologies with secondary school students reflects this fact. For example, researchers are keen to investigate how socially oriented tools and technologies—such as social networking sites, online games, or cell phones—might play a role in supporting language learning, both in and outside the classroom. Web 2.0 tools may, at first blush, seem to provide ideal spaces in which adolescent language learners can develop a range of language skills as well as intercultural and social skills; however, when a close look is taken at how they are actually used by teachers, 'little evidence of groundbreaking activities' or of students developing 'criticality, self-management and metacognitive reflection' is found (Luckin et al., 2008, p. 6). Clearly, the role of the teacher and the design of activities play a major part in whether a specific tool helps or hinders language learning. In addition, in some cases, teenagers simply do not want the social tools that they use as an essential part of their out-of-school lives to be appropriated in formal learning contexts (Crook, Fisher, Graber, Harrison, & Lewin, 2008).

Given the wide range of factors that affect the use of technologies in different contexts, it is difficult to generalize from studies that focus purely on learning outcomes, such as the effect of SMS messaging on vocabulary acquisition—hence the often contradictory findings in what may appear to be similar studies. With the social turn in language learning research (see Chapter 2), researchers have become increasingly interested in these wider factors, and many studies that we examined in this chapter take into account constructs that are difficult to pin down, such as learners' motivation, engagement, and perceptions. From our review of these studies, it would appear that the jury is still out on the question of whether learning technologies improve language learning outcomes for adolescents. The simple answer is that sometimes they do and sometimes they do not; it depends on a very wide range of factors which are particular to each individual context, and even to each individual learner.

5

Learning Languages with Technology: What We Know Now

Preview

In this chapter, we will return to the statements about learning technologies that you responded to in Activity 1.1. For each statement, I will provide a response based on the research that has been reviewed in this book. Before you read my responses, review your own ideas by returning to your responses in Activity 1.1.

Activity 5.1: Review your opinions

In Activity 1.1 (page 7), you indicated how strongly you agreed with some statements about learning a language with technology. Before you continue reading this chapter, go back and complete the questionnaire again. Compare the responses you gave then to those you would give now. Have your views about learning technologies been changed or confirmed by what you have read in the preceding chapters?

Reflecting on Ideas about Learning Technologies: Learning from Research

1 If teachers use technology with young learners, they also need to pay attention to issues like e-safety.

Most educational curricula for primary and secondary school learners encourage teachers to work with their students on digital literacy issues such as e-safety. Topics frequently covered with primary school learners include learning how to search safely online, to avoid strangers online, and to be aware of the negative effects of cyberbullying. Teenagers are frequently more autonomous users of technology than younger learners, and although issues of cyberbullying are still relevant, complex age-related issues such as sexting can be of additional concern to parents and teachers of adolescents.

Within some school curricula—for example, in many UK schools—there has been a move away from blocking students' access to the internet, seeking instead to enable access while teaching students to be responsible digital citizens who use online resources appropriately. Overall, there is agreement that educators need to help students navigate an increasingly digital world effectively and safely, and that this pertains to teachers across all subject areas, with both primary and secondary school students.

2 Tools like blogs and wikis can help students improve their writing skills.

Web 2.0 tools like blogs and wikis have long been considered potentially beneficial for students in developing their writing skills. Students can write for a real audience in blogs and therefore write with a real communicative purpose. Students can also interact with their readership via a blog's comments section. These are all seen as advantages to using blogs over pen and paper for writing. Although much of the research into the use of blogs supports the notion that students become more *motivated* to write in the foreign language, it is less clear to what extent the *quality* of their writing actually improves. Students with a lower level of language proficiency, for example, may benefit less from the use of blogs than stronger students in some contexts (Sercu, 2013). Nevertheless, the majority of research into blogs does point to positive results in the development of literacy, and in some cases, blogs can help learners reposition themselves as 'good' writers and as valued members of the class (for example, Danzak, 2011).

The social nature of wikis has been found to support collaborative writing practices, with several studies reporting on how students review and improve on each other's texts in wikis. The key to the successful use of wikis in the language classroom appears to rest on ensuring that relevant and effective tasks are set, so that the potential for learners to support each other's writing is fully exploited.

3 Teachers need training to be able to use technology effectively with students.

As we have seen from the research studies examined in this volume, there are many factors involved when we attempt to assess the ability of technologies to support language learning. Key factors include local context, technological infrastructure, students' attitudes and motivation, task design, the learning beliefs that underpin the design of learning tasks, and, not least, the extent to which teachers have received training. Effective teacher training is crucial to the successful deployment of learning technologies in a wide range of contexts, from the use of interactive whiteboards to the One Laptop per Child (OLPC) initiative.

Mishra and Koehler's TPACK model (2006) provides a useful framework within which to situate the role of teacher training in developing teachers' ICT competence. TPACK stands for Technological Pedagogical Content Knowledge; it suggests that teachers need not only *content* knowledge— knowing what to teach—and *pedagogical* knowledge—knowing how to teach content—but also *technological* knowledge—knowing how to choose the best technologies to support learning outcomes and how to deploy these technologies effectively.

4 Governments should provide funding to schools to buy the latest educational technologies.

Although government funding for new technologies in schools sounds like a good idea in theory, in practice it is sometimes misguided. The issue with focusing on buying hardware—or educational software—in order to improve learning is that these decisions are often guided by political rather than educational thinking. The example of interactive whiteboards is salutary: significant amounts of money have been spent by governments around the world on these expensive pieces of equipment, but there is no research available to show that the presence of an interactive whiteboard in a classroom leads to improved learning outcomes. A similar approach has been seen with the OLPC initiative in developing countries, where the provision of low-cost laptops to primary and secondary school students is seen as an investment that will automatically lead to better learning. However, research shows that it is spending money on improving school buildings, training teachers, and providing appropriate pedagogical materials, not on the latest hardware, that leads to improved learning outcomes (Warschauer & Ames, 2010).

The latest wave of techno-centric thinking promotes the use of tablets— often preloaded with tutorial CALL learning materials—as a way to improve low test scores, despite little evidence to support this. Having a clear rationale for tablet implementation, as well as access to reliable infrastructure and support, long-term planning, teacher training, and the involvement of all stakeholders, is crucial to the successful implementation of these devices in schools.

5 Technology depersonalizes learning.

Depending on how one defines the term 'personalize' and on how technology is used, one could indeed claim that technology depersonalizes learning.

For example, research with some of the blended models currently being popularized in North America, such as those employed in schools like Rocketship Education elementary schools or Carpe Diem (see Classroom Snapshot 4.1), shows mixed learning results. The tutorial CALL principles underlying these models, in which learners interact with adaptive learning programs preloaded onto computers in schools, can discourage an inquiry-based, problem-solving approach to learning materials (Warschauer, 2011). In addition, despite claims that such models lead to improved test scores for primary and secondary school students, it appears that these test scores decline over time as the effects of novelty wear off.

However, learners sitting in front of terminals and individually interacting with computer programs is just one of the many ways that technology can be used in schools. As many of the studies described in this volume show, technology can also engage and motivate learners, provide innovative opportunities for communication and interaction, and in some cases lead to improved learning outcomes.

6 Learners communicate only with machines and not with each other if they are using technology in the classroom.

Like our previous question, this depends on how the technology is used. In some cases, teachers may want to use computer programs or games to support students' learning or to improve test scores. We saw that tablets with learning materials can support SEN young learners and adolescents. On the other hand, we saw that even when children use games that are designed to help them prepare for a standardized test like the *Jidō Eiken* in Japan (see Classroom Snapshot 1.1), playing these games does not necessarily translate into improved test scores for students. Thus, we have seen situations in which learners do indeed communicate only with machines and not with each other in the classroom. However, we have also seen many situations and studies in which technology is used to support and develop communication skills, in reading, writing, listening, and speaking, with both young learners and adolescents.

In addition, technology may provide a medium for communication in a second or foreign language where no other option exists. For example, in Classroom Snapshot 1.2, we saw how videoconferencing technology is used to bring qualified English language teachers into rural classrooms in Uruguay, giving underprivileged children access to English language classes that they would otherwise not receive.

7 Technology games, such as vocabulary or grammar games, can improve learning outcomes.

There is, indeed, evidence that some so-called serious or educational games can lead to gains in vocabulary (Sundqvist, 2009), as well as support the use of certain communicative strategies, such as information-seeking, strategizing, socializing, and problem-solving, for some adolescent learners (Li et al., 2014). However, not all games are created equal. The research appears most promising when considering how adolescent learners interact in MMORPGs. These offer immersive 3D environments with demanding game-based tasks that require communication between players via both text and speech, providing meaningful contexts for social interaction through dialog. It appears that adolescents who are already gamers benefit most from these types of games, and the amount of time they spend playing a MMORPG—which means being exposed to English in a real communicative context—is a key factor.

Another key factor is the type of game. For example, immersive 3D single-player games that require minimal communication, like *The Sims*, do not appear to support language acquisition to the same extent that multiplayer communicative games like *World of Warcraft* do. However, not all adolescents are enamored of complex games, and some students can become demotivated if the game is overly challenging. In addition, it appears that games that are based on tutorial CALL principles, in which learners interact with the computer rather than with each other, do not always lead to improved outcomes in language learning (see Classroom Snapshot 1.1).

8 Technology can effectively support students with special educational needs.

Most research into the potential of assistive technologies to support SEN learners at primary and secondary school has taken place in a range of subject areas, not just language arts, and results are indeed promising. Tablets, for example, have been taken up enthusiastically by teachers working with SEN learners due to their multimodal and tactile assistive qualities, as well as the growing range of educational apps available for SEN students. Tablets have been found to support literacy development in autistic children and also to increase SEN students' engagement with learning materials, improve their social interaction skills, and develop their academic and communicative skills.

Research into the effectiveness of assistive technologies for SEN primary and secondary school students who are also ELLs appears to support these findings on the whole, although there is less research available. One major challenge is that ELLs with SEN are either not diagnosed at all or are wrongly diagnosed as having SEN rather than language challenges. However, the research that does exist with SEN ELLs suggests that, depending on the learning materials or apps used and on task design, learners' engagement with language learning materials can increase. It also suggests that language arts teachers generally have a positive attitude to the use of assistive technologies with SEN primary and adolescent language learners.

9 Young learners and adolescents are naturally good at using new technologies.

Although young learners and adolescents are frequently referred to as 'digital natives' (Prensky, 2001), research has shown that this is a myth. Young people are not automatically effective users of new technologies. Although they may be confident with new technologies and use many socially oriented technologies for friendship-driven purposes, they are not always effective users of new technologies. They may be adept at using social networking sites and apps to socialize with friends, but they are less able to search effectively for information online or to evaluate the veracity or provenance of that information. In short, they can be confident but uncritical users of technology. Large-scale research studies (for example, see Spotlight Study 2.1) have shown that the ICT skills of young learners and adolescents depend on a wide range of factors. For example, the impact of home and school contexts and students' individual characteristics have been found to affect their digital literacies. Parents' educational level and profession, the number of books in the home, and access to ICT resources at home are all examples of factors in the home that can affect young learners' and adolescents' ICT skills. Whether learners receive ICT instruction in school is another factor that affects their digital literacies.

10 Technologies like cell phones should be kept out of the language classroom as they don't teach, they distract.

This is certainly a fear that many teachers and parents may have about technologies like cell phones. Pedagogical, technological, and classroom management issues come into play with cell phones. For example, when teachers have a clear pedagogical rationale for the use of cell phones with students, as well as the necessary technological infrastructure and classroom management strategies in place, they can be used effectively (see Hockly & Dudeney, 2014).

Research into the effectiveness of cell phones to support learning with young learners and adolescents shows mixed results. For instance, some vocabulary acquisition studies show learning gains (for example, Hwang, Chen, Shadiev, Huang, & Chen, 2014; Tabatabaei & Goojani, 2012), whereas other studies point to factors such as students having additional time to be exposed to the language, rather than the effect of mobile devices themselves, as the key factor affecting learning (Sandberg et al., 2011; Hwang & Chen, 2013). Other research shows that students do not necessarily want to read texts on cell phones and may prefer paper (Huang & Lin, 2011). Similarly, the delivery of learning games like crosswords via mobile devices rather than on paper leads to no significant difference in learning outcomes—in this case, it is the game itself that is the motivating factor, rather than the mode of delivery (Hung et al., 2009). In short, cell phones can aid learning in some cases, but in others, factors beyond the technology appear to have a greater effect on learning outcomes. It is very difficult to ascribe the success or failure of learning to a specific device, as it depends on the context in which it is used, the task type, and students' motivation, among other factors.

Conclusion

To what extent, then, do learning technologies support English language acquisition? This is the question that needs to be answered, given the amount of money that is spent on educational technologies by governments, schools, teachers, parents, and students, and the amount of hype that is created by technology providers who suggest that technologies are a 'solution' to education. The short answer is: the jury is still out. As we have seen in this volume, the effectiveness—or lack of effectiveness—of a particular technology, software, or technology-based learning approach depends on a wide range of factors that extend well beyond the technology itself. In some cases, and for some students, research shows that technology can indeed support learning outcomes in some areas of language acquisition. However, in other cases, there is no direct correlation between a specific learning technology and learning outcomes. As such, a statement such as 'technology *x* helps students learn English' is misguided at best, and deliberately misleading at worst. It simply flies in the face of the evidence. Where does this leave teachers? On the one hand, we need to resist techno-centric views of learning technologies as silver bullets that will somehow magically lead to improved learning outcomes for our students. On the other hand, we need to accept that technology is an integral part of our digital world and a key aspect of our students' lives. Ignoring technology completely, or pretending that it has nothing to do with language learning or teaching, is unrealistic. Instead, we should ensure that our own use of learning technologies with our students, both in and outside the classroom, is based on a sound understanding of the research and thoughtfully integrated into a sound pedagogy. Only then can we hope to engage in a principled use of learning technologies to support our students' language development, whatever their age, whatever needs they may have, and whatever our teaching context.

Suggestions for Further Reading

With a rich research tradition dating back several decades, there is a wealth of literature available about technology in language learning. Much of it relates to research and there are also books available for teachers on pedagogical practice. The recommended titles below focus primarily on research and provide a good foundation for understanding the past, present, and possible futures of learning technologies in our field.

boyd, d. (2014). *It's complicated: The social lives of networked teens.* Yale, CT: Yale University Press.

Social media scholar danah boyd has spent over a decade working with US adolescents, collecting detailed information on how they use technologies in their daily lives. Through a range of case studies of teenagers from various ethnic and socioeconomic backgrounds, in this volume she provides a nuanced and illuminating picture of how technologies are woven into North American teenagers' development of self and their communications with others. Writing in an accessible and engaging style, she explodes some of the myths that surround adolescents' use of current technologies and provides a scholarly and in-depth exploration of how adolescence is affected by the use of social and networked media.

Farr, F., & Murray, L. (Eds.). (2016). *Routledge handbook of language learning and technology.* New York, NY: Routledge.

This 38-chapter volume provides a thorough state-of-the-art overview of technology in second language learning. Chapters are written by researchers and experts in the field, and a wide range of issues is explored. The volume opens with three chapters dedicated to the historical and conceptual background to CALL research, and continues with chapters on core CALL issues such as teacher education, materials development, research, digital literacies, and testing and evaluation, among others. Research into specific technologies such as IWBs, mobile devices, virtual worlds, and social networks is considered, and there are sections dedicated to game-based learning, to the role of corpora and data-driven learning, and to CALL learning resources. This volume is highly recommended for those interested in a thorough and up-to-date introduction to a rich variety of CALL research areas.

Kerr, P. (2014). *Adaptive learning.* The Round Publishing.

This short, well-written volume, available as a free e-book, provides a useful introduction to adaptive learning software, which is becoming increasingly ubiquitous in schools that advocate a blended learning approach to core subjects like English and math. Taking a critical stance, Kerr highlights the political and economic interests that drive the current interest in adaptive learning, and describes how it works in English language learning. This is an excellent read for those who are unfamiliar with adaptive learning and how it works, or interested in why significant economic investment in adaptive learning is currently taking place and what this might mean for the future of language learning.

Selwyn, N. (2014). *Distrusting educational technology: Critical questions for changing times.* London: Routledge.

Selwyn provides an informed and thoughtful critique of the unquestioning acceptance of educational technology as something that automatically helps children learn. Skeptical of the techno-centrism and techno-solutionism that underlies much of the public discourse surrounding learning technologies, he advocates a questioning stance that identifies the wide range of economic, social, and political issues underlying the widespread and frequently uncritical adoption of learning technologies in education. It is essential reading for those who wish to learn more about the wider ramifications of technology in education and to better understand the complex nexus of factors that often affect technology adoption in schools, colleges, and universities.

Thomas, M., Reinders, H., & Warschauer, M. (Eds.). (2013). *Contemporary computer-assisted language learning.* London: Bloomsbury.

The 19 chapters in this volume cover a wide range of current CALL-related topics, and were written by researchers and experts in each area. Each chapter provides a contemporary account of research and developments in the field, and topics covered include language testing, teacher education, CALL materials design, online learning, virtual worlds, digital games, and mobile language learning, as well as issues such as CALL and less commonly taught languages, and CALL and learner autonomy. It is highly recommended for those who wish to gain an overview of recent research and developments in the field, across a range of CALL areas.

Ware, P., & Hellmich, E. A. (2014). CALL in the K–12 context: Language learning outcomes and opportunities. *CALICO Journal, 31,* 1–18.

This article summarizes some of the key research that has taken place into the use of learning technologies with primary and secondary school students, primarily in North America but also in international contexts. Ware and Hellmich divide their review of the research into two areas: research that focuses on learning *outcomes*—that is, the use of technologies to improve test scores as a way to measure language learning—and learning *opportunities*—that is, the use of technologies to enhance language learning. This article provides a good starting point for those wishing to review key K–12 learning technologies research.

Warschauer, M. (2011). *Learning in the cloud: How (and why) to transform schools with digital media.* New York, NY: Teachers College Press.

Warschauer is one of the foremost researchers into the use of learning technologies to support language and literacy development in US schools. In this volume, he describes how technologies have been used in a number of US schools in successful—and less successful—ways. From the failed One Laptop per Child (OLPC) initiative in Birmingham Public Schools in Alabama to the successful implementation of laptops in a new inquiry-oriented, project-based curriculum to support writing and literacy for ELLs in Littleton Public Schools, Warschauer reviews a range of research carried out with learning technologies in elementary, middle, and high schools. This book provides a useful, readable, and evidence-based review of how and when learning technologies can and do support learning outcomes, and also when they do not.

Glossary

action research: research that focuses on and explores specific areas through practice, often carried out in the classroom.

adaptive learning: the use of algorithms in technology to adapt learning content based on the user's prior experiences of success or failure with similar content.

apps: short for 'applications'; software programs found on mobile devices.

assistive touch: an accessibility feature of mobile devices that enables physically impaired users to utilize simplified gestures with a touch screen, for example, tapping instead of swiping.

asynchronous: communication that takes place over a period of time, for example, via email or discussion forums; contrasts with *synchronous*.

augmented reality: a technology that superimposes information onto the user's environment, for example, by accessing the camera of a mobile device and providing an augmented or enhanced experience of reality.

avatar: a figure or icon that represents a person online, for example in a computer game or as a user's online profile.

blended learning: learning that takes place partly face to face in the classroom, and partly online via a computer or mobile device.

blog: an online journal or diary. Postings appear in reverse chronological order on the blog page.

Bluetooth: a technology that allows for short-range wireless connections between mobile devices.

cell phone: a mobile phone.

chatbot: an artificial intelligence *avatar* or robot that can carry out conversations with a human interlocutor online.

cloud computing: computer servers that allow users to store their information online rather than on their own personal devices.

cognitive load: the amount of mental effort required by one's working memory when processing information at a given time.

Common European Framework of Reference (CEFR): a framework used in Europe and internationally to provide a common definition of language competences at six different levels.

communicative competence: a term used in linguistics to refer to grammatical, syntactical, and phonological knowledge, as well as to a person's ability to use language appropriately in social contexts.

communicative language teaching (CLT): an L2 teaching approach that highlights language as a communicative system and emphasizes the use of real-life situations.

content-based language teaching (CBLT): instruction provided to students who are learning both the academic content and the language in which the content is taught.

convenience sampling: the selection of research participants based on their convenience and accessibility to the researcher.

cyberbullying: bullying that takes place via digital communication, for example through intimidating or threatening text messages.

design-based research: a research methodology that aims to bridge theory and practice by using theoretical principles to examine the effects of the design—for example, of learning materials or approaches—on practice.

digital artifact: a digital product, or an outcome in digital format, that is created by teachers and/or students.

ecological perspective: a research perspective that attempts to take into account a wide array of factors, including social, historical, cultural, psychological, environmental, and cognitive aspects.

English as a Foreign Language (EFL): the teaching of English to people for whom it is not the first language and who live in a country where English is not ordinarily spoken.

English as a Second Language (ESL): the teaching of English to people for whom it is not the first language and who live in a country where English is ordinarily spoken.

English Language Learner (ELL): a term often used in the US context to describe a learner of English as a second language.

e-reader: a device for reading electronic books.

Facebook: a public social networking site.

filter bubble: the intellectual isolation that results from search engines using algorithms to select the information a user is exposed to based on their interests, past search behavior, and location, thereby isolating them from information that may contradict their viewpoints.

first language (L1): the language that was acquired first in a person's life.

fitness tracker: a device or program used to measure health-related information such as calorie consumption, quantity and quality of sleep, and distance walked or run.

foreign language: a language that is not ordinarily spoken among people in a learner's local environment.

formative assessment: formal and informal assessment procedures used to measure ongoing student learning.

games console: an electronic device used for playing computer games.

geotagging: the process of adding geographical metadata to *digital artifacts*.

GPS tracking: the process of identifying one's location through the Global Positioning System, which can pinpoint one's longitude and latitude, and, if moving, one's ground speed and direction.

human–computer interaction: the study of how humans interact with computers, and how technology design can affect this interaction.

hyperlinking: the use of electronic links in a digital document that allow one to move to another point in the same document, or to another web page.

hypertext: digital text which contains links to other texts.

informalization: the increasingly informal nature of relationships and communication between individuals, reflected in informal choices of language.

information gap task: a language learning task in which individuals have different pieces of information and need to communicate with each other in order to find the missing information.

information overload: a sense of being overwhelmed by too much information, typically brought on by the huge amount of information available online.

Instagram: a social networking site based on photo sharing.

instant messaging: a program or app that allows users to exchange text messages in real time.

integrated skills approach: an approach to teaching the four skills—reading, writing, speaking, and listening—at the same time, typically through project work where all the skills are deployed at some point in the same piece of work.

intelligent assistant: a program or app that performs personal services and tasks for the user, such as sending an email, adding items to a calendar, or reminding the user of events.

interactive fiction: a story in which the reader makes choices that will take the narrative in different directions depending on their choices.

interactive whiteboard (**IWB**): a large digital board, typically mounted at the front of a classroom and connected to a computer. Users can interact with the board's surface by using a digital stylus, keyboard, or, in some cases, their fingers.

jigsaw task: a language learning task in which students have different pieces of information that they need to share and that together form a whole.

L1: see 'first language'.

L2: see 'second language' and 'foreign language'.

lexis: another word for vocabulary.

language arts: the term used in the USA to refer to what in other contexts might be called 'subject English'; instruction in language and literature.

Learning Management System (**LMS**): a program that supports the delivery of online courses by allowing for administration, documentation, and the tracking of student activity and achievement.

mediation: from Vygotsky; the process by which a child interacts socially with others and through which learning occurs.

microblogging: an electronic medium that allows for short texts to be shared with others. Twitter is a well-known current microblogging platform.

Massively Multiplayer Online Role-Playing Game (**MMORPG**): an online game in which large numbers of players take part simultaneously and that typically takes place in a 3D virtual world.

MP3 player: a digital audio player.

MP4 player: a digital video player.

Multimedia Messaging Service (**MMS**): a standard way of sending short messages that can include text, audio, images, and video.

multiliteracies: a new approach to literacy that takes into account our increasingly digital world and includes the ability to communicate effectively via digital media and in digital environments.

natural language processing: the ability of computers to understand and process human speech.

netbook: a small laptop.

online discussion forum: an online space in which users can post content such as text, images, and video, and where others can reply.

open source software: software whose source code is publicly available to be modified by anyone.

Personal Digital Assistant (PDA): a small handheld device capable of performing functions such as voice recording, email, or web searching.

plug-in: a component that adds features to an existing computer program.

podcast: digital media, often in the form of an audio recording, that is broadcast periodically and can be downloaded from the internet onto a computer or mobile device.

pragmatic meaning: the implied meaning of an utterance rather than its literal meaning.

process approach: an approach to teaching writing that encourages students to draft, review, reformulate, and redraft written work.

psycholinguistics: the study of the psychological and cognitive processes involved in language acquisition.

purposeful sampling: the careful and deliberate selection of specific participants for research.

qualitative research: research that focuses on naturally occurring behaviors using data that are primarily descriptive and non-numeric.

quantitative research: research that focuses on the manipulation of variables and uses data that are numerically quantified and statistically analyzed.

random sampling: the selection of research participants to represent a random sample of the population under study.

second language (L2): a language learned after the first language (L1) has been acquired.

second language acquisition (SLA): both the process by which an individual learns a second language, and the actual study of that process.

Second Life: a 3D virtual world launched by Linden Labs in 2003.

sexting: the sending of sexually explicit messages or photographs by cell phone.

Short Message Service (SMS): the industry-standard service that allows users to send text messages from one digital device to another.

The Sims: a life simulation video game in which players create virtual characters called 'Sims', place them in homes, help direct their moods, and take care of them.

Siri: an *intelligent assistant* developed by Apple for its iPhone, iPod, and iPad products.

situated learning: learning that takes place in informal social contexts via meaningful interactions.

Skype: a computer program that enables telephone calls to be made via the internet with or without video.

smartphone: a cell phone that typically has a touch screen interface, connects to the internet, and allows the user to download *apps*.

smart watch: a small digital device worn on the wrist that has functionality very similar to that of a *smartphone*.

social constructivist: based on a theory of learning that emphasizes the role of social interaction and cultural context in the creation of knowledge.

social networking site: a website that allows users to create online networks by contacting others and to share content with their online network.

speech-to-text: a computer program that transforms human speech into written text.

summative assessment: formal and informal assessment procedures used to measure student achievement.

superdiversity: the multiple forms of social and cultural differentiation that exist within many of today's urban areas, caused by rapidly changing patterns of migration due to globalization.

supermobility: the increased mobility of languages, both geographically and in the development of new genres, due to globalization and the internet.

synchronous: communication that takes place in real time, for example, via instant messaging or voice chat; contrasts with *asynchronous*.

systemic functional linguistics: an approach to linguistics that considers the relationship between language and its use in social settings, developed by Halliday.

tablet: a small portable computer with a touch screen interface.

text-to-speech: a computer program that transforms written text into speech.

tutorial CALL: an approach to computer-assisted language learning in which students interact with pre-programmed content, such as text-reconstruction or fill-in-the-blank activities.

videoconferencing equipment: a telecommunications technology which allows communication between users in two or more locations via text, audio, and video.

Virtual Learning Environment (**VLE**): a platform or online space which includes discussion forums, text chat and/or videoconferencing features, assessment and grading features, student tracking, etc.

virtual world: a 3D digital world in which users can take on an *avatar* and interact with others and the environment.

voice recognition software: a computer program that can recognize and transcribe or react to human speech.

voice response system: an automated telephone-based software that responds to voice commands, for example, by routing calls to different locations or by providing specific responses based on the caller's voice input.

WebQuest: an inquiry-oriented, project-based lesson that requires students to find and synthesize information from a range of online sources.

wiki: a series of editable web pages.

working memory: a part of short-term memory where information is temporarily stored and managed to allow for cognitive processing.

Zone of Proximal Development (**ZPD**): from Vygotsky; refers to how children can succeed at tasks that may be beyond their immediate capacity with the help and guidance of more knowledgeable or experienced others.

References

Abbitt, J., & Ophus, J. (2008). What we know about the impacts of WebQuests: A review of research. *AACE Journal, 16*, 441–56.

Abraham, L. (2008). Computer-mediated glosses in second language reading comprehension and vocabulary learning: A meta-analysis. *Computer-Assisted Language Learning, 21*, 199–226.

Alberta Government. (2012). *Bring your own device: A guide for schools.* Edmonton: Alberta Education.

Alberta Government. (2013). *Learning and technology policy framework. Policy Direction 5: Access, infrastructure and digital learning environments.* Retrieved January 27 2016 from http://www.education.alberta.ca/admin/technology/policyframework/policy5.aspx

Alemi, M., Sarab, M., & Lari, Z. (2012). Successful learning of academic word list via MALL: Mobile assisted language learning. *International Education Studies, 5*, 99–109.

Alias, N., DeWitt, D., Siraj, S., Kamaruddin, S., & Daud, M. (2013). A content analysis of wikis in selected journals from 2007 to 2012. *Social and Behavioral Sciences, 103*, 28–36.

Alliance for Childhood (2012). *Facing the screen dilemma: Young children, technology and early education.* Boston, MA: Campaign for a Commercial-Free Childhood; New York, NY: Alliance for Childhood.

Ariew, R., & Ercetin, G. (2004). Exploring the potential of hypermedia annotations for second language reading. *Computer Assisted Language Learning, 17*, 237–59.

Banegas, D. (2013). ELT through videoconferencing in primary schools in Uruguay: First steps. *Innovation in Language Learning and Teaching, 7*, 179–88.

Barbour, M. K. (2014). State of the nation: K–12 online learning in Canada. *Intercambio, 6*, 27.

Baron, N. S. (2008). *Always on: Language in an online and mobile world.* New York, NY: Oxford University Press.

Barton, D., & Lee, C. (2013). *Language online: Investigating digital texts and practices.* London: Routledge.

Bawden, D. (2008). Origins and concepts of digital literacy. In C. Lankshear & M. Knobel (Eds.), *Digital literacies: Concepts, policies and practices* (pp. 17–32). New York, NY: Peter Lang.

Bax, S. (2003). CALL – Past, present and future. *System, 31*, 13–28.

Belshaw, D. (2011). *What is digital literacy? A pragmatic investigation.* (Unpublished Ed.D thesis). University of Durham.

Belz, J., & Thorne, S. (Eds.). (2006). *Internet-mediated intercultural foreign language education*. Boston, MA: Heinle and Heinle.

Blattner, G., & Fiori, M. (2009). Facebook in the language classroom: Promises and possibilities. *International Journal of Instructional Technology and Distance Learning, 6,* 17–28.

Block, D. (2003). *The social turn in second language acquisition*. Georgetown, DC: Georgetown University Press.

Blood, R. (2000, September 7). Weblogs: A history and perspective. [Blog post.] Retrieved January 27 2016 from http://www.rebeccablood.net/essays/weblog_history.html

boyd, d. (2014). *It's complicated: The social lives of networked teens*. Yale, CT: Yale University Press.

boyd, d., & Ellison, N. B. (2007). Social network sites: Definition, history, and scholarship. *Journal of Computer-Mediated Communication, 13,* 210–30.

Brandl, K. (2002). Integrating internet-based reading materials into the foreign language curriculum: From teacher- to student-centered approaches. *Language Learning and Technology, 6,* 87–107.

Braun, S. (2007). Integrating corpus work into secondary education: From data-driven learning to needs-driven corpora. *ReCALL, 19,* 307–28.

Brovetto, C. (in press). Language policy and language practice in Uruguay. A case of innovation in English language teaching in primary schools. In L. D. Kamhi-Stein, G. Díaz Maggioli, & L. C. de Oliveira (Eds.), *English language teaching in South America: Policy, preparation, and practices*. Clevedon: Multilingual Matters.

Bryant, T. (2006). Using World of Warcraft and other imports to foster a targeted, social and cooperative approach toward language learning. Academic Commons. Retrieved January 27 2016 from https://web.archive.org/web/20061013063948/http://www.academiccommons.org/commons/essay/bryant-MMORPGs-for-SLA

Burr, E., Haas, E, & Ferriere, K. (2015). *Identifying and supporting English learner students with learning disabilities: Key issues in the literature and state practice*. Institute of Education Sciences. US Department of Education. Retrieved January 27 2016 from: http://ies.ed.gov/ncee/edlabs

Byron, T. (2010). *Do we have safer children in a digital world? Review of progress since the 2008 Byron Review*. Nottingham: DCSF Publications.

Campigotto, R., McEwen, R., & Demmans Epp., C. (2013). Especially social: Exploring the use of an iOS application in special needs classrooms. *Computers and Education, 60,* 74–86.

Canale, M., & Swain, M. (1980). Theoretical bases of communicative approaches to second language teaching and testing. *Applied Linguistics, 1,* 1–47.

Canuel, M. (2013). Foreword. In M. K. Barbour, *State of the nation: K–12 online learning in Canada* (pp. 3–4). Retrieved January 27 2016 from http://www.openschool.bc.ca/pdfs/state_of_nation-2013.pdf

Carr, N. (2010). *The shallows: What the internet is doing to our brains*. New York, NY: W.W. Norton & Company.

Chalfen, R. (2009). 'It's only a picture': Sexting, 'smutty' snapshots and felony charges. *Visual Studies, 24,* 258–68.

Chapelle, C. A. (1997). CALL in the year 2000: Still in search of research paradigms? *Language Learning & Technology, 1,* 19–43.

Chapelle, C. A. (1999). Research questions for a CALL research agenda: A reply to Rafael Salaberry. *Language Learning & Technology, 3,* 108–13.

Chapelle, C. (2005). Interactionist SLA theory in CALL research. In J. L. Egbert & G. M. Petrie, *CALL research perspectives* (pp. 53–64). Mahwah, NJ: Lawrence Erlbaum Associates.

Chapelle, C. A. (2008). Utilizing technology in language assessment. In E. Shohamy (Ed.), *Encyclopedia of language education, second edition* (pp. 23–34). Heidelberg: Springer.

Chen, C.-M., & Li, Y.-L. (2010). Personalized context-aware ubiquitous learning system for supporting effective English vocabulary learning. *Interactive Learning Environments, 18,* 341–64.

Christensen, C. M., Horn, M. B., & Johnson, C. W. (2008). *Disrupting class: How disruptive innovation will change the way the world learns.* New York, NY: McGraw-Hill.

Chu, S. K. W., Wong, K., Lee, C., Chow, K., & Ng, J. (2011). *Inquiry project-based learning with wiki at Primary Five level.* Paper presented at CITE Research Symposium, The University of Hong Kong.

Chun, D. M., & Plass, J. L. (1996). Facilitating reading comprehension with multimedia. *System, 24,* 503–19.

Chun, D. M., & Plass, J. L. (1997). Research on text comprehension in multimedia environments. *Language Learning & Technology, 1,* 60–81.

Cilesiz, S. (2009). Educational computer use in leisure contexts: A phenomenological study of adolescents' experiences at internet cafés. *American Educational Research Journal, 46,* 232–74.

Clark, D. (2013, March 11). Negroponte: 10 reasons why his Ethiopian project smacks of Educational Colonialism. Plan B Blog. [Blog post.] Retrieved January 27 2016 from http://donaldclarkplanb.blogspot.co.uk/2013/03/negroponte-10-reasons-why-his-ethiopian.html

Clark, W., & Luckin, R. (2013). *What the research says: iPads in the classroom.* London: London Knowledge Lab and Institute of Education, University of London.

Cooney, G., & Keogh, K. (2007). *Use of mobile phones for language learning and assessment for learning.* Paper presented at MLearn, 2007.

Cope, B., & Kalantzis, M. (Eds.). (2000). *Multiliteracies: Literacy learning and the design of social futures.* London: Routledge.

Crook, C., Fisher, T., Graber, R., Harrison, C., & Lewin, C. (2008). *Implementing Web 2.0 in secondary schools: Impacts, barriers, and issues.* Coventry: BECTA.

Crystal, D. (2006). *Language and the internet, second edition.* Cambridge: Cambridge University Press.

Crystal, D. (2011). *Internet linguistics: A student guide.* London: Routledge.

Cuban, L. (2015a, May 19). Coding for kids: the new vocational education. [Blog post.] Retrieved January 27 2016 from https://larrycuban.wordpress.com/2015/05/19/coding-for-kids-the-new-vocational-education/

Cuban, L. (2015b, February 9). The lack of evidence-based practice: The case of classroom technology (Part 2). [Blog post.] Retrieved January 27 2016 from https://larrycuban.wordpress.com/2015/02/09/the-lack-of-evidence-based-practice-the-case-of-classroom-technology-part-2/

Cuban, L. (2015c, June 6). District purchasing of high-tech devices: How teachers continue to lose out. [Blog post.] Retrieved January 27 2016 from https://larrycuban.wordpress.com/2015/06/06/district-purchasing-of-high-tech-devices-how-teachers-continue-to-lose-out/

Cuban, L. (2015d, February 12). The lack of evidence-based practice: The case of classroom technology (Part 3). [Blog post.] Retrieved January 27 2016 from https://larrycuban.wordpress.com/2015/02/12/the-lack-of-evidence-based-practice-the-case-of-classroom-technology-part-3/

Cuellar, R., de la Colina, M., Episcopo, V., Hollier, D., & Leavell, J. (2009). A study of an online reading intervention for secondary English language learners. *National Forum of Teaching Educational Journal, 19*, 1–15.

Cumming, T. M., & Draper Rodriguez, C. (2013). Integrating the iPad into language arts instruction for students with disabilities: Engagement and perspectives. *Journal of Special Education Technology, 28*, 43–52.

Danzak, R. (2011). Defining identities through multiliteracies: EL teens narrate their immigration experiences as graphic stories. *Journal of Adolescent & Adult Literacy, 55*, 187–96.

Davies, A., Fidler, D., & Gorbis, M. (2011). *Future work skills 2020*. Palo Alto, CA: University of Phoenix Research Institute.

de Oliveira, L. C., & Schleppegrell, M. J. (2015). *Focus on grammar and meaning*. Oxford: Oxford University Press.

Ducate, L., & Arnold, N. (Eds.). (2006). *Calling on CALL: From theory and research to new directions in foreign language teaching*. San Marcos, TX: CALICO.

Ducate, L., & Lomicka, L. (2005). Exploring the blogosphere: Uses of weblogs in the foreign language classroom. *Foreign Language Annals, 38*, 410–21.

Dudeney, G. (2006). Interactive, quite bored. *IATEFL CALL Review, Summer 2006*, 8–9.

Dudeney, G., & Hockly, N. (2012). ICT in ELT: How did we get here and where are we going? *English Language Teaching Journal, 66*, 533–42.

Dudeney, G., Hockly, N., & Pegrum, M. (2013). *Digital literacies*. London: Routledge.

Egbert, J. L., & Petrie, G. M. (Eds.). (2005). *CALL research perspectives*. Mahwah, NJ: Lawrence Erlbaum Associates.

Elliot, N., Ruggles Gere, A., Gibson, G., Toth, C., Whithaus, C., & Presswood, A. (2013). *Uses and limitations of automated writing evaluation software, WPA (Council of Writing Program Administrators), CompPile Research Bibliographies, 23*. Retrieved January 27 2016 from http://comppile.org/wpa/bibliographies/Bib23/AutoWritingEvaluation.pdf

Enyedy, N. (2014). *New interest, old rhetoric, limited results, and the need for a new direction for computer-mediated learning*. Boulder, CO: National Education Policy Center.

Farr, F., & Murray, L. (Eds.). (2016). *Routledge handbook of language learning and technology*. New York, NY: Routledge.

Flanigan, R. L. (2014, March). Taking the pulse of digital literacy. *Education Week,* 30–2.

Foreman, J. (2004). Video game studies and the emerging instructional revolution. *Innovate Journal of Online Education, 1.*

Fraillon, J., Ainley, J., Schulz, W., Friedman, T., & Gebhardt, E. (2013). *Preparing for life in a digital age. The IEA International Computer and Information Literacy Study international report.* Cham: Springer.

Fritschi, J., & Wolf, M. A. (2012). *Turning on mobile learning in North America: Illustrative initiatives and policy implications.* Paris: UNESCO.

Fu, D., & Matoush, M. M. (2015). *Focus on literacy.* Oxford: Oxford University Press.

Funk, J., Brouwer, J., Curtiss, K., & McBroom, E. (2009). Parents of preschoolers: Expert media recommendations and ratings knowledge, media-effects beliefs, and monitoring practices. *Pediatrics, 123,* 981–8.

Gambrell, L. (2005). Reading literature, reading text, reading the internet: The times they are a'changing. *The Reading Teacher, 58,* 588–91.

Gebhard, M., Shin, D. S., & Seger, W. (2011). Blogging and emergent L2 literacy development in an urban elementary school: A functional perspective. *CALICO Journal, 28,* 278–307.

Gee, J. P. (2012). Foreword. In H. Reinders (Ed.), *Digital games in language learning and teaching* (pp. xii – xiv). Basingstoke: Palgrave Macmillan.

Geist, M. (2013, November 1). *Statscan data points to Canada's growing digital divide.* Retrieved January 27 2016 from http://www.thestar.com/business/tech_news/2013/11/01/statscan_data_points_to_canadas_growing_digital_divide_geist.html

Gillen, J. (2014). *Digital literacies.* London: Routledge.

Gillespie, A. A. (2011). *Child pornography: Law and policy.* New York, NY: Routledge.

Goodfellow, R., & Lamy, M.-N. (2009). Introduction: A frame for the discussion of learning cultures. In R. Goodfellow & M.-N. Lamy (Eds.), *Learning cultures in online education* (pp. 1–14). London: Continuum.

Goto Butler, Y., Someya, Y., & Fukuhara, E. (2014). Online games for young learners' foreign language learning. *English Language Teaching Journal, 63,* 265–75.

Government of Saskatchewan. (2013). Learning resources evaluation guidelines. Saskatchewan Ministry of Education. Retrieved January 27 2016 from http://www.education.gov.sk.ca/learning-resource-evaluation-guidelines

Grant, L. (2009). *Learning in families: A review of research evidence and the current landscape of learning in families with digital technologies.* Bristol: Futurelab. Retrieved January 27 2016 from http://archive.futurelab.org.uk/resources/documents/project_reports/becta/Learning_in_Families_educators_report.pdf

Gray, L., Thomas, N., & Lewis, L. (2010). *Teachers' Use of Educational technology in U.S. public schools: 2009. (NCES 2010-040).* Washington, DC: National Center for Education Statistics, Institute of Education Sciences, U.S. Department of Education.

Gregg, K. (1993). Taking explanation seriously; or, Let a couple of flowers bloom. *Applied Linguistics, 14,* 276–94.

Grimes, D., & Warschauer, M. (2010). Utility in a fallible tool: A multi-site case study of automated writing evaluation. *Journal of Technology, Language, and Assessment, 8,* 1–43.

Guo, Z., & Stevens, K. J. (2011). Factors influencing perceived usefulness of wikis for group collaborative learning by first year students. *Australasian Journal of Educational Technology, 27,* 221–42.

Hague, C., & Williamson, B. (2009). *Digital participation, digital literacy and school subjects: A review of policies, literature and evidence.* Bristol: Futurelab. Retrieved January 27 2016 from http://www.nfer.ac.uk/publications/FUTL08/FUTL08_home.cfm

Haight, M., Quan-Haase, A., & Corbett, B.A. (2014). Revisiting the digital divide in Canada: The impact of demographic factors on access to the internet, level of online activity, and social networking site usage. *Information, Communication & Society, 17,* 503–19.

Hall, I., & Higgins, S. (2005). Primary school students' perceptions of interactive whiteboards. *Journal of Computer Assisted Language Learning, 21,* 102–17.

Hall, R., Atkins, L., & Fraser, J. (2014). Defining a self-evaluation digital literacy framework for secondary educators: The DigiLit Leicester project. *Research in Learning Technology, 22,* 21440. Retrieved January 27 2016 from http://dx.doi.org/10.3402/rlt.v22.21440

Harrison, R., & Thomas, M. (2009). Identity in online communities: Social networking sites and language learning. *International Journal of Emerging Technologies and Society, 7,* 109–24.

Hendron, J. G. (2003). Educators as content publishers. *The VSTE Journal, 17,* 2–6.

Hill, L. (2010). *Finding a voice in the digital classroom: The effects of asynchronous discussion on language acquisition and communication apprehension among secondary ESOL students in South Texas.* (Unpublished Ed.D thesis). Texas A&M University–Corpus Christi.

Hockly, N. (2013a). Interactive Whiteboards. *English Language Teaching Journal, 67,* 354–8.

Hockly, N. (2013b). Designer learning: The teacher as designer of mobile-based classroom learning experiences. *The International Research Foundation for English Language Education.* Retrieved January 27 2016 from http://www.tirfonline.org/english-in-the-workforce/mobile-assisted-language-learning/designer-learning-the-teacher-as-designer-of-mobile-based-classroom-learning-experiences/

Hockly, N., & Clandfield, L. (2010). *Teaching Online: Tools and techniques, options and opportunities.* Guildford: Delta Publishing.

Hockly, N., & Dudeney, G. (2014). *Going Mobile: Teaching with hand-held devices.* Guildford: Delta Publishing.

Holland, V. M., Kaplan, J. D., & Sams, M. R. (Eds.). (1995). *Intelligent language tutors: Theory shaping technology.* Mahwah, NJ: Lawrence Erlbaum Associates.

Horn, M. B., & Staker, H. (2011). *The rise of K–12 blended learning.* Innosight Institute. Retrieved January 27 2016 from http://www.christenseninstitute.org/wp-content/uploads/2013/04/The-rise-of-K-12-blended-learning.pdf

Hourigan, T., & Murray, L. (2010). Using blogs to help language students to develop reflective strategies: Towards a pedagogical framework. *Australasian Journal of Educational Technology, 26,* 209–25.

Huang, L.-L., & Lin, C.-C. (2011). EFL learners' reading on mobile phones. *The JALT CALL Journal, 7,* 61–78.

Hubbard, P. & Levy, M. (2016). Theory in computer-assisted language learning research and practice. In F. Farr & L. Murray (Eds.), *Routledge handbook of language learning and technology* (pp. 24–38). New York, NY: Routledge.

Hubbard, P. (Ed.). (2009). *Computer assisted language learning (Vols I–IV). Critical Concepts in Linguistics series*. New York, NY: Routledge.

Hung, H.-C., Young, S., & Lin, C.-P. (2009). Constructing the face-to-face collaborative game-based interacted environment for portable devices in English vocabulary acquisition. In A. Dimitracopoulou, C. O'Malley, D. Suthers & P. Reimann (Eds.), *Proceedings of the 8th International Conference on Computer Supported Collaborative Learning* (pp. 370–5). Rhodes: University of the Aegean.

Hwang, W.-Y., & Chen, H. (2013). Users' familiar situational contexts facilitate the practice of EFL in elementary schools with mobile devices. *Computer Assisted Language Learning, 26,* 101–25.

Hwang, W.-Y., Chen, H., Shadiev, R., Huang, R. Y.-M., & Chen, C.-Y. (2014). Improving English as a foreign language writing in elementary schools using mobile devices in familiar situational contexts. *Computer Assisted Language Learning, 27,* 359–78.

International Society for Technology Education. (2007). National Educational Technology Standards for Students (NETS). Retrieved February 3 2016 from http://www.iste.org/standards/iste-standards/standards-for-students

Irwin, C., Ball, L., Desbrow, B., & Leveritt, M. (2012). Students' perceptions of using Facebook as an interactive learning resource at university. *Australasian Journal of Educational Technology, 28,* 1221–32.

Ito, M., Baumer, S., Bittani, M., boyd, d., Cody, R., Herr-Stephenson, B., Horst, H. A., Lange, P. G., Mahendran, D., Martinez, K. Z., Pascoe, C. J., Perkel, D., Robinson, L., Sims, C., Tripp, L. (2009). *Hanging out, messing around, geeking out: Living and learning with new media*. Cambridge, MA: MIT Press.

Jang, E. E. (2014). *Focus on assessment*. Oxford: Oxford University Press.

Jarvis, H., & Achilleos, M. (2003). From computer assisted language learning (CALL) to mobile assisted language use (MALU). *TESL-EJ, 16,* 1–18.

Jarvis, H., & Krashen, S. (2014). Is CALL obsolete? Language acquisition and language learning revisited in a digital age. *TESL-EJ, 17,* 1–6.

Johnson, L., Adams, S., & Cummins, E. (2012). *NMC Horizon Report: 2012 K–12 Edition*. Austin, TX: New Media Consortium. Retrieved January 27 2016 from http://www.nmc.org/pdf/2012-horizon-report-K12.pdf

Kagohara, D. M., van der Meer, L., Ramdoss, S., O'Reilly, M. F., Lancioni, G. E., Davis, T. N., Rispoli, M., et al. (2013). Using iPods and iPads in teaching programs for individuals with developmental disabilities: A systematic review. *Research in Developmental Disabilities, 34,* 147–56.

Kárpáti, A. (2009). Web 2 technologies for net native language learners: A "social CALL". *ReCALL, 21,* 139–56.

Kennedy, G., Dalgarno, B., Bennett, S., Gray, K., Waycott, J., Judd, T., Bishop, A., Maton, K., Krause, K.-L., & Chang, R. (2009). *Educating the Net generation: A handbook of findings for practice and policy*. Australian Learning and Teaching Council. Retrieved January 27 2016 from https://web.archive.org/web/20151011044456/http://netgen.unimelb.edu.au/downloads/handbook/NetGenHandbookAll.pdf

Kern, R., & Warschauer, M. (2000). Introduction: Theory and practice of network-based language teaching. In M. Warschauer & R. Kern (Eds.), *Network-based language teaching: Concepts and practice* (pp. 1–19). Cambridge: Cambridge University Press.

Kerr, P. (2014). *Adaptive learning.* The Round Publishing. Retrieved January 27 2016 from http://the-round.com/resource/a-short-guide-to-adaptive-learning-in-english-language-teaching/

Kim, H.-S. (2010). Three teachers' initial efforts to use Twitter for teaching English in public schools. *Multimedia-Assisted Language Learning, 13,* 129–54.

Kramsch, C. (Ed.). (2002). *Language acquisition and socialization.* Oxford: Oxford University Press.

Kramsch, C., & Steffensen, S. V. (2008). Ecological perspectives on second language acquisition and socialization. In P. A. Duff & N. H. Hornberger (Eds.), *Encyclopedia of language and education, second edition, Volume 8: Language socialization* (pp. 17–28). New York, NY: Springer.

Kramsch, C., & Thorne, S. L. (2002). Foreign language learning as global communicative practice. In D. Block & D. Cameron (Eds.), *Globalization and language teaching* (pp. 83–100). London: Routledge.

Kukulska-Hulme, A., & Shield, L. (2007). An overview of mobile assisted language learning: Can mobile devices support collaborative practice in speaking and listening? *ReCALL, 20,* 1–20.

Lafer, G. (2014). *Do poor kids deserve lower-quality education than rich kids? Evaluating school privatization proposals in Milwaukee, Wisconsin.* Washington, DC: Economic Policy Institute.

Lan, Y.-J., Sung, Y.-T., & Chang, K.-E. (2007). A mobile-device-supported peer-assisted learning system for collaborative early EFL reading. *Language Learning and Technology, 11,* 130–51.

Lan, Y.-J., Sung, Y.-T., & Chang, K.-E. (2009). Let us read together: Development and evaluation of a computer assisted reciprocal early English reading system. *Computers & Education, 5,* 1188–98.

Lan, Y.-J., Sung, Y.-T., & Chang, K.-E. (2013). From particular to popular: Facilitating EFL mobile-supported cooperative reading. *Language Learning and Technology, 17,* 23–38.

Lanier, J. (2010). *You are not a gadget.* New York, NY: Vintage Books.

Laurillard, D. (2008). *Digital technologies and their role in achieving our ambitions for education.* London: Institute of Education.

Laurillard, D. (2012). *Teaching as a design science: building pedagogical patterns for learning and technology.* New York, NY: Routledge.

Lee, Y. J., & Gerber, H. (2013). It's a WoW world: Second language acquisition and massively multiplayer online gaming. *Multimedia-Assisted Language Learning, 16,* 53–70.

Lenhart, A. (2015). *Teens, Social Media and Technology Overview 2015.* Pew Research Center. Retrieved January 27 2016 from http://www.pewinternet.org/files/2015/04/PI_TeensandTech_Update2015_0409151.pdf

Levine, A., Ferenz, O., & Reves, T. (2000). EFL academic reading and modern technology: How can we turn our students into independent critical readers? *TESL-EJ, 4,* 1–9.

Levy, M. (2013). Foreword. In M. Thomas, H. Reinders, & M. Warschauer (Eds.), *Contemporary computer-assisted language learning* (pp. xvii–xix). London: Bloomsbury.

Levy, M. (2016). Researching in language learning and technology. In F. Farr & L. Murray (Eds.), *Routledge handbook of language learning and technology* (pp. 101–14). New York, NY: Routledge.

Levy, M., & Hubbard, P. (2005). Why call CALL 'CALL'? *Computer Assisted Language Learning, 18,* 143–9.

Levy, M., & Kennedy, C. (2005). Learning Italian via mobile SMS. In A. Kukulska-Hulme & J. Traxler (Eds.), *Mobile learning: A handbook for educators and trainers,* (pp. 76–83). London: Taylor and Francis.

Levy, M., & Stockwell, G. (2006). *CALL dimensions: Options and issues in computer-assisted language learning.* Mahwah, NJ: Erlbaum.

Lewis, M. (1993). *The lexical approach: The state of ELT and the way forward.* Hove: Language Teaching Publications.

Li, J. (2009). The evolution of vocabulary learning strategies in a computer-mediated reading environment. *CALICO Journal, 27,* 118–46.

Li, Z., Chiu, C.-C., & Coady, M. R. (2014). The transformative power of gaming literacy: What can we learn from adolescent English language learners' literacy engagement in World of Warcraft (WoW)? In H. R. Gerber & S. Schamroth Abrams (Eds.). *Bridging literacies with videogames* (pp. 129–52). Boston, MA: Sense Publishers.

Liebtag, E. (2013). Moving forward with Common Core State Standards implementation: Possibilities and potential problems. *Journal of Curriculum and Instruction, 7,* 56–70.

Lightbown, P. M. (2014). *Focus on content-based language teaching.* Oxford: Oxford University Press.

Lightbown, P. M., & Spada, N. (2013). *How languages are learned, fourth edition.* Oxford: Oxford University Press.

Lin, C., & Tseng, Y. (2012). Videos and animations for vocabulary learning: A study on difficult words. *The Turkish Online Journal of Educational Technology, 11,* 346–56.

Lin, C.-H., & Warschauer, M. (2015). Online foreign language education: What are the proficiency outcomes? *The Modern Language Journal, 99,* 394–7.

Lin, C.-C., & Yu, Y.-C. (2012). Learning English vocabulary on mobile phones. In J. Colpaert, A. Aerts, W.-C. V. Wu, & Y.- C. J. Chao (Eds.), *The medium matters* (pp. 416–20). Proceedings from the 15th International CALL Conference.

Linn, S. (2012). *Healthy kids in a digital world: A strategic plan to reduce screen time for children 0–5 through organizational policy and practice change.* Report by the Campaign for a Commercial-Free Childhood for Kaiser Permanente Community Health Initiatives Grants Program. Retrieved January 27 2016 from http://www.commercialfreechildhood.org/healthykidsdigitalworld

Llosa, L., & Slayton, J. (2009). Using program evaluation to inform and improve the education of young English language learners in US schools. *Language Teaching and Research, 13,* 35–54.

Looker, E. D., & Thiessen, V. (2003). *The digital divide in Canadian schools: Factors affecting student access to and use of information technology.* Canadian Education Statistics Council (CESE).

Lu, M. (2008). Effectiveness of vocabulary learning via mobile phone. *Journal of Computer Assisted Learning, 24,* 515–25.

Lück, K. (2008). Web-based foreign language reading: Affective and productive outcomes. *CALICO Journal, 25,* 305–25.

Luckin, R., Logan, K., Clark, W., Graber, R., Oliver, M., & Mee, A. (2008). *KS3 and KS4 learners use of web 2.0 technologies in and out of school.* Coventry: BECTA.

Lund, A. (2008). Wikis: A collective approach to language production. *ReCALL, 20,* 35–54.

Lwo, L., & Chia-Tzu Lin, M. (2012). The effects of captions in teenagers' multimedia L2 learning. *ReCALL, 24,* 188–208.

Mak, B., & Coniam, D. (2008). Using wikis to enhance and develop writing skills among secondary school students in Hong Kong. *System, 36,* 437–55.

Mawer, K., & Stanley, G. (2011). *Digital play: Computer games and language aims.* Guildford: DELTA Publishing.

Mazer, J. P., Murphy, R. E., & Simonds, C. J. (2007). I'll see you on "Facebook": The effects of computer-mediated teacher self-disclosure on student motivation, affective learning, and classroom climate. *Communication Education, 56,* 1–17.

McGrail, E., & Davis, A. (2011). The influence of classroom blogging on elementary student writing. *Journal of Research in Childhood Education, 25,* 415–37.

McEnery, T., & Xiao, R. (2011). What corpora can offer in language teaching and learning. In E. Hinkel (Ed.), *Handbook of research in second language teaching and learning, Volume II* (pp. 364–80). London: Routledge.

Melhuish, K., & Falloon, G. (2010). Looking to the future: M-learning with the iPad. *Computers in New Zealand Schools: Learning, Leading, Technology, 22,* 1–16.

Merchant, G. (2007). Writing the future in the digital age. *Literacy, 41,* 118–28.

Meskill, C. & Quah, J. (2013). Researching language learning in the age of social media. In M. Thomas, H. Reinders, & M. Warschauer (Eds.), *Contemporary computer-assisted language learning* (pp. 39–54). London: Bloomsbury.

Miller, D., & Glover, D. (2010). Interactive whiteboards: A literature survey. In M. Thomas and E. Cutrim Schmid (Eds.), *Interactive whiteboards for education: Theory, research and practice* (pp. 1–19). New York, NY: IGI Global.

Mishra, P., & Koehler, M. J. (2006). Technological pedagogical content knowledge: A framework for teacher knowledge. *Teachers College Record, 108,* 1017–54.

Mitchell, R., Myles, F., & Marsden, E. (2013). *Second language learning theories, third edition.* New York, NY: Routledge.

Morton, H., Gunson, N., & Jack, M. (2012). Interactive language learning through speech-enabled virtual scenarios. *Advances in Human–Computer Interaction.* Retrieved January 27 2016 from http://dx.doi.org/10.1155/2012/389523

Morton, H., & Jack, M. (2010). Speech interactive computer-assisted language learning: A cross-cultural evaluation. *Computer Assisted Language Learning, 23,* 295–319.

Moss, G., & Jewitt, C. (2010). Policy, pedagogy and interactive whiteboards: What lessons can be learnt from early adoption in England? In M. Thomas and E. Cutrim Schmid (Eds.), *Interactive whiteboards for education: Theory, research and practice* (pp. 20–36). New York, NY: IGI Global.

Mueller, T. G., Singer, G. H. S., & Carranza, F. D. (2006). A national survey of the educational planning and language instruction practices for students of moderate to severe disabilities who are English language learners. *Research and Practice for Persons with Severe Disabilities, 31,* 242–54.

Murray, L., & Hourigan, T. (2005). *Identifying roles for blogs in SLA.* Paper presented at UNTELE: Input, interaction, feedback, evaluation, second language acquisition and multimedia environments, L'Université de Technologie de Compiègne, France.

Nation, I. S. P. (2001). *Learning vocabulary in another language.* Cambridge: Cambridge University Press.

Ngowi, R. (2014, October 1). App teaches kindergartners basic computer coding. *The Huffington Post.* Retrieved January 27 2016 from http://www.huffingtonpost.com/2014/10/01/coding-app-kindergarten_n_5913602.html

Oakley, G., Howitt, C., Garwood, R., & Durack, A.-R. (2013). Becoming multimodal authors: Pre-service teachers' interventions to support young children with autism. *The Australian Journal of Early Childhood, 38,* 86–96.

O'Dowd, R. (Ed.). (2007). *Online intercultural exchange: An introduction for foreign language teachers.* Clevedon: Multilingual Matters.

O'Dowd, R. (2014). Telecollaboration and CALL. In M. Thomas, H. Reinders, & M. Warschauer (Eds.), *Contemporary computer-assisted language learning* (pp. 123–39). London: Bloomsbury.

O'Dowd, R., & Ritter, M. (2006). Understanding and working with 'failed communication' in telecollaborative exchanges. *CALICO Journal, 23,* 623–42.

Oliver, K., Kellogg, S., & Patel, R. (2012). An investigation into reported differences between online foreign language instruction and other subject areas in a virtual school. *CALICO Journal, 22,* 513–36.

Oliver, R., & Philp, J. (2015). *Focus on oral interaction.* Oxford: Oxford University Press.

O'Reilly, T. (2004). What is web 2.0: design patterns and business models for the next generation of software. Retrieved January 27 2016 from http://www.im.ethz.ch/education/HS08/OReilly_What_is_Web2_0.pdf

Oxford, R. (1995). Linking theories of learning with intelligent computer-assisted language learning (ICALL). In V. M. Holland, J. D. Kaplan, & M. R. Sams (Eds.), *Intelligent language tutors: Theory shaping technology* (pp. 359–69). Mahwah, NJ: Lawrence Erlbaum Associates.

Palmer, D. S. (2010). *Second language pragmatic socialization in World of Warcraft.* (Unpublished PhD thesis). University of California.

Parker, L. L. (2008). Technology in support of young English learners in and out of school. In L. L. Parker (Ed.), *Technology-mediated learning environments for young English learners: Connections in and out of school* (pp. 213–50). New York, NY: Lawrence Erlbaum Associates.

Payne, J. S., & Ross, B. M. (2005). Synchronous CMC, working memory, and L2 oral proficiency development. *Language Learning & Technology, 9,* 35–54.

Payne, J. S., & Whitney P. J. (2002). Developing L2 oral proficiency through synchronous CMC: Output, working memory, and interlanguage development. *CALICO Journal, 20,* 7–32.

Payne, M. (2005). The digital divide and its discontents. *Currents in Electronic Literacy, 9.* Retrieved January 27 2016 from http://currents.dwrl.utexas.edu/fall05/payne.html

Payton, S., & Hague, C. (2010). *Digital literacy in practice: Case studies of primary and secondary classrooms.* Bristol: Futurelab. Retrieved January 27 2016 from http://www2.futurelab.org.uk/resources/documents/project_reports/digital_literacy_case_studies.pdf

Peck, C., Kappler Hewitt, K., Mullen, C., Lashley, C., Eldridge, J., & Douglas, T.-R. M. O. (2015). Digital youth in brick and mortar schools: Examining the complex interplay of students, technology, education, and change. *Teachers College Record, 117,* 1–40.

Pegrum, M. (2009). *From blogs to bombs: The future of digital technologies in education.* Crawley, Australia: UWA Publishing.

Pegrum, M. (2010). 'I link, therefore I am': Network literacy as a core digital literacy. *E-learning and Digital Media, 7,* 346–54.

Pegrum, M. (2014). *Mobile learning: Languages, literacies and cultures.* Basingstoke: Palgrave Macmillan.

Pegrum, M. (2015). Language and literacies for digital lives. In E. Martín-Monje, I. Elorza, & B. García Riaza (Eds.), *Technological advances in specialized linguistic domains: Learning on the move* (pp. 16–36). London: Routledge.

Peterson, M. (2012). Language learner interaction in a massively multiplayer online role-playing game. In H. Reinders (Ed.), *Digital games in language learning and teaching* (pp. 70–92). Basingstoke: Palgrave Macmillan.

Pew Research Center. (2014a). *Older adults and technology use.* Retrieved January 27 2016 from http://www.pewinternet.org/files/2014/04/PIP_Seniors-and-Tech-Use_040314.pdf

Pew Research Center. (2014b). *Internet user demographics.* Retrieved January 27 2016 from http://www.pewinternet.org/data-trend/internet-use/latest-stats/

Picardo, J. (2008, 25 June). Using Voki and a blog in a sequence of three lessons. [Blog post.] Retrieved January 27 2016 from http://www.boxoftricks.net/2008/06/using-voki-and-a-blog-in-a-sequence-of-three-lessons/

Plester, B., & Wood, C. (2009). Exploring relationships between traditional and new media literacy is: British preteen texters at school. *Journal of Computer-Mediated Communication, 14,* 1108–29.

Plowman, L., & McPake, J. (2013). Seven myths about young children and technology. *Child Education, 89,* 27–33.

Prensky, M. (2001). Digital natives, digital immigrants. *On the Horizon, 9,* 1–6.

Raith, T. (2009). The use of weblogs in language education. In Thomas, M. (Ed.), *Handbook of research on web 2.0 and second language learning* (pp. 274–91). Hershey, PA: IGI Global.

Rand Corporation. (2014). *Interim Research on Personalized Learning*. Bill & Melinda Gates Foundation. Retrieved January 27 2016 from http://collegeready. gatesfoundation.org/wp-content/uploads/2015/06/Early-Progress-on-Personalized-Learning-Full-Report.pdf

Reedy, G. (2008). PowerPoint, interactive whiteboards, and the visual culture of technology in schools. *Technology, Pedagogy and Education, 1*, 143–62.

Reinders, H. (2012). *Digital games in language learning and teaching*. Basingstoke, UK: Palgrave Macmillan.

Reinhardt, J., & Zander, V. (2011). Social networking in an intensive English program classroom: A language socialization perspective. *CALICO Journal, 28*, 326–44.

Reinking, D. (2005). Multimedia learning of reading. In R. E. Mayer (Ed.), *Cambridge handbook of multimedia learning* (pp. 355–74). Cambridge: Cambridge University Press.

Rich, M. (2014, January 24). Screen time study finds education drop-off. *The New York Times*. Retrieved January 27 2016 from http://www.nytimes.com/2014/01/24/us/screen-time-study-finds-education-drop-off.html

Richards, J., & Rodgers, T. (2014). *Approaches and methods in language teaching, third edition*. Cambridge: Cambridge University Press.

Rideout, V. (2014). *Learning at home: families' educational media use in America*. The Joan Ganz Cooney Center. Retrieved February 3 2016 from http://files.eric.ed.gov/fulltext/ED555586.pdf

Rideout, V., Foehr, U. G., & Roberts, D. F. (2010). *Generation M²: Media in the lives of 8- to 18-year-olds*. Menlo Park, CA: Kaiser Family Foundation.

Ring, C., & LaMarche, M. (2012). Mobile technology and communication. *ABA Literature Summary E-Newsletter, 10. Special Learning*.

Sadler, R., & Dooly, M. (2014). Language learning in virtual worlds: Research and practice. In M. Thomas, H. Reinders, & M. Warschauer (Eds.), *Contemporary computer-assisted language learning* (pp. 159–82). London: Bloomsbury.

Sakar, A., & Ercetin, G. (2005). Effectiveness of hypermedia annotations for foreign language reading. *Journal of Computer Assisted Learning, 21*, 28–38.

Salaberry, R. (1999). CALL in the year 2000: still developing the research agenda. *Language Learning & Technology, 3*, 104–7.

Salaway, G., & Caruso, J. (2008). The ECAR study of undergraduate students and information technology. Boulder, CO: EDUCAUSE.

Sandberg, J., Maris, M., & de Geus, K. (2011). Mobile English learning: An evidence-based study with fifth graders. *Computers & Education, 57*, 1334–47.

Satar, H. M., & Özdener, N. (2008). The effects of synchronous CMC on speaking proficiency and anxiety: Text versus voice chat. *The Modern Language Journal, 92*, 595–613.

Savignon, S., & Roithmeier, W. (2004). Computer-mediated communication: Texts and strategies. *CALICO Journal, 21*, 265–90.

Schubert, A., & Wurf, G. (2014). Adolescent sexting in schools: Criminalisation, policy imperatives, and duty of care. *Issues in Educational Research, 24*, 190–211.

Selwyn, N. (2011). *Education and technology: Key issues and debates.* London: Continuum International.

Selwyn, N. (2013). *Education in a digital world: Global perspectives on technology and education.* London, Routledge.

Selwyn, N. (2014). *Distrusting educational technology: Critical questions for changing times.* London: Routledge.

Sercu, L. (2013). Weblogs in foreign language education: Real and promised benefits. *Proceedings of INTED2013, 7th International Technology, Education and Development Conference, Valencia, Spain,* 4355–66.

Shenton, A., & Pagett, L. (2007). From "bored" to screen: The use of the interactive whiteboards for literacy in six primary classrooms in England. *Literacy, 41,* 129–36.

Shipton, L. (2011). *Improving e-safety in primary schools: A guidance document.* Sheffield: Sheffield Hallam University.

Siemens, G. (2005). Connectivism: A learning theory for the digital age. *Journal of Instructional Technology and Distance Learning, 2,* 3–10.

Sigman, A. (2012). Time for a view on screen time. *Archives of Disease in Childhood.* Retrieved January 27 2016 from http://adc.bmj.com/content/early/2012/09/04/archdischild-2012-302196.extract

Silverman, R., & Hines, S. (2009). The effect of multimedia-enhanced instruction on vocabulary of English-language learners and non-English-language learners in pre-kindergarten through second grade. *Journal of Educational Psychology, 2,* 305–14.

Simpson, J., & Walker, A. (2014). New technologies for English language learning and teaching. In C. Leung & B. Street (Eds.), *The Routledge Companion to English Studies* (pp. 475–89). London: Routledge.

Sinclair, J. (1988). Foreword. In D. Willis & J. Willis, *The Collins COBUILD English Course* (p. i). London: Collins ELT.

Soars, L., Soars, J., & Davies, G. (2009). *New Headway Pre-Intermediate Third Edition iTools.* Oxford: Oxford University Press.

Solvie, P. (2004). The digital whiteboard: A tool in early literacy instruction. *The Reading Teacher, 57,* 484–7.

Souleles, N. (2012). Perceptions of undergraduate graphic design students on the educational potential of Facebook. *Research in Learning Technology, 20,* 241–52.

Squire, K. (2005). Changing the Game: What Happens When Video Games Enter the Classroom? *Innovate Journal of Online Education, 1,* 1–20.

Stanley, G. (2013). *Language learning with technology: Ideas for integrating technology in the classroom.* Cambridge: Cambridge University Press.

Stanley, G. (2015). Plan Ceibal English: Remote teaching of primary school children in Uruguay through videoconferencing. In C. N. Giannikas, L. McLaughlin, G. Fanning & N. Deutsch Muller (Eds.), *Children learning English: From research to practice* (pp. 201–13). Reading: Garnet.

Stockwell, G. (Ed.). (2012). *Computer-assisted language learning: Diversity in research and practice.* Cambridge: Cambridge University Press.

Suh, S., Kim, S. W., & Kim, N. J. (2010). Effectiveness of MMORPG-based instruction in elementary English education in Korea. *Journal of Computer Assisted Learning, 26,* 370–8.

Sundqvist, P. (2009). *Extramural English matters: Out-of-school English and its impact on Swedish ninth graders' oral proficiency and vocabulary*. Karlstad: Karlstad University Studies.

Sweller, J. (2005). Implications of cognitive load theory for multimedia learning. In R. E. Mayer (Ed.), *The Cambridge handbook of multimedia learning* (pp. 19–30). Cambridge: Cambridge University Press.

Tabatabaei, O., & Goojani, A. (2012). The impact of text messaging on vocabulary learning of Iranian EFL learners. *Cross Cultural Communication, 8*, 47–55.

Takeuchi, L. (2011). *Families matter: Designing media for a digital age*. New York, NY: The Joan Ganz Cooney Center.

Tamim, R. M., Borokhovski, E., Pickup, D., & Bernard, R. M. (2015). *Large-scale, government-supported educational tablet initiatives*. Burnaby: Commonwealth of Learning.

Thomas, M., & Cutrim Schmid, E. (Eds.). (2010). *Interactive whiteboards for education: Theory, research and practice*. New York, NY: IGI Global.

Thomas, M., Reinders, H., & Warschauer, M. (Eds.). (2013). *Contemporary computer-assisted language learning*. London: Bloomsbury.

Thorne, S. L. (2003). Artifacts and cultures-of-use in intercultural communication. *Language Learning and Technology, 7*, 38–67.

Thorne, S. L. (2008). Transcultural communication in open internet environments and massively multiplayer online games. In S. Magnan (Ed.), *Mediating discourse online* (pp. 305–27). Amsterdam: Benjamins.

Thorne, S. L. (2009). 'Community', semiotic flows, and mediated contribution to activity. *Language Teaching, 42*, 81–94.

Thorne, S. L. (2010). The 'intercultural turn' and language learning in the crucible of new media. In F. Helm & S. Guth (Eds.), *Telecollaboration 2.0: Language, literacies and intercultural learning in the 21st century* (pp. 139–64). Bern: Peter Lang.

Thorne, S. L., & Black, R. (2007). Language and literacy development in computer-mediated contexts and communities. *Annual Review of Applied Linguistics, 27*, 133–60.

Thorne, S. L., & Reinhardt, J. (2008). "Bridging Activities," New Media Literacies, and Advanced Foreign Language Proficiency. *CALICO Journal, 25*, 558–72.

Thornton, P., & Houser, C. (2002). M-learning: Learning in transit. In P. Lewis (Ed.), *The changing face of CALL* (pp. 229–43). Lisse: Swets and Zeitlinger.

Trucano, M. (2012, March 23). Evaluating one laptop per child (OLPC) in Peru. [Blog post.] Retrieved January 27 2016 from http://blogs.worldbank.org/edutech/olpc-peru2

Twiner, A. (2010). Interactive whiteboards and the discourses of transformation, affordance, orchestration and participation. In M. Thomas and E. Cutrim Schmid (Eds.), *Interactive whiteboards for education: Theory, research and practice* (pp. 37–52). New York, NY: IGI Global.

van Dijck, J., & Nieborg, D. (2009). Wikinomics and its discontents: A critical analysis of web 2.0 business manifestos. *New Media & Society, 11*, 855–74.

van Lier, L. (2004a). *The ecology and semiotics of language learning. A sociocultural perspective*. Dordrecht: Kluwer.

van Lier, L. (2004b). The semiotics and ecology of language learning: Perception, voice, identity and democracy. *Utbildning & Demokrati, 13,* 79–103.

Voosloo, S. (2012). *Mobile learning and policies: Key issues to consider.* Paris: UNESCO.

Wachnuk, K. (2013). *Learning for All K–12 regional project report: Rainbow District School Board.* Ontario Ministry of Education. Retrieved January 27 2016 from http://www.edu.gov.on.ca/eng/general/elemsec/speced/RainbowDSB2011_13.pdf

Walker, A., & White, G. (2013). *Technology enhanced language learning: Connecting theory and practice.* Oxford: Oxford University Press.

Wang, S., & Vásquez, C. (2012). Web 2.0 and second language learning: What does the research tell us? *CALICO Journal, 29,* 412–30.

Ware, P., & Hellmich, E. A. (2014). CALL in the K–12 context: Language learning outcomes and opportunities. *CALICO Journal, 31,* 1–18.

Ware, P., & Kessler, G. (2014). Telecollaboration in the secondary language classroom: Case study of adolescent interaction and pedagogical integration. *Computer Assisted Language Learning.* Retrieved January 27 2016 from http://www.tandfonline.com/doi/abs/10.1080/09588221.2014.961481

Warschauer, M. (1996). Computer assisted language learning: An introduction. In S. Fotos (Ed.), *Multimedia language teaching* (pp. 3–20). Tokyo: Logos International.

Warschauer, M. (2002). Reconceptualizing the digital divide. *First Monday, 7.* Retrieved January 27 2016 from http://firstmonday.org/ojs/index.php/fm/article/view/967/888/

Warschauer, M. (2005). Sociocultural perspectives on CALL. In J. L. Egbert & G. M. Petrie (Eds.), *CALL research perspectives* (pp. 41–51). Mahwah, NJ: Lawrence Erlbaum Associates.

Warschauer, M. (2011). *Learning in the cloud: How (and why) to transform schools with digital media.* New York, NY: Teachers College Press.

Warschauer, M., & Ames, M. (2010). Can one laptop per child save the world's poor? *Journal of International Affairs, 64,* 33–51.

Warschauer, M., Cotton S., & Ames, M. (2012). One laptop per child Birmingham: Case study of a radical experiment. *International Journal of Learning and Media, 3,* 61–76.

Warschauer, M., & Grimes, D. (2008). Automated writing assessment in the classroom. *Pedagogies, 3,* 52–67.

Warschauer, M., & Healey, D. (1998). Computers and language learning: An overview. *Language Teaching, 31,* 57–71.

Warschauer, M., Knobel, M., & Stone, L. (2004). Technology and equity in schooling: Deconstructing the digital divide. *Educational Policy, 18,* 562–88.

Warschauer, M., & Matuchniak, T. (2010). New technology and digital worlds: Analyzing evidence of equity in access, use, and outcomes. *Review of Research in Education, 34,* 179–225.

Watters, A. (2014, December 9). Ed-Tech Year in Review. Model View Culture. [Blog post.] Retrieved January 27 2016 from https://modelviewculture.com/pieces/ed-tech-year-in-review

Watters, A. (2015, March 1). Moving beyond personalized education. Hack Education. [Blog post.] Retrieved January 27 2016 from http://hackeducation.com/2015/03/01/moving-beyond-personalized-instruction/

Wenglinsky, H. (2005). *Using technology wisely: The keys to success in schools*. New York, NY: Teachers College Press.

White, G. (1998). *Listening*. Oxford: Oxford University Press.

Whyte, S. (2011). Learning to teach with videoconferencing in primary foreign language classrooms. *ReCALL, 23*, 271–93.

Winer, D. (2003, June 8). What are weblogs? [Blog post.] Retrieved January 27 2016 from http://bgbg.blogspot.com.es/2003_06_08_bgbg_archive.html#200402733

Wong, L.-H., & Looi, C.-K. (2010). Vocabulary learning by mobile-assisted authentic content creation and social meaning-making: Two case studies. *Computer-Assisted Learning, 26*, 421–33.

Woo, M., Chu, S., Ho, A., & Li, X. (2011). Using a wiki to scaffold primary-school students' collaborative writing. *Educational Technology & Society, 14*, 43–54.

Wood, R., & Ashfield, J. (2008). The use of the interactive whiteboard for creative teaching and learning in literacy and mathematics: a case study. *British Journal of Educational Technology, 39*, 84–96.

Woods, P. (2014). Do laptops in schools promote learner autonomy and achievement in English language learning? In T. Pattison, *IATEFL 2013: Liverpool conference selections* (pp. 128–9). Faversham: IATEFL.

Woolfolk, A. E. (2012). *Educational Psychology, 12th edition*. Harlow: Pearson.

Yáñez, L., & Coyle, Y. (2010). Children's perceptions of learning with an interactive whiteboard. *English Language Teaching Journal, 65*, 446–57.

Yang, Y., & Egbert, J. (2004). Mediating the digital divide in CALL classrooms: Promoting effective language tasks in limited technology contexts. *ReCALL, 16*, 280–91.

Yeok-Hwa Ngeow, K. (2010). Restricted internet access and censorship: CALL alternatives and initiatives. In J. Egbert (Ed.), *CALL in limited technology contexts* (pp. 93–106). San Marcos, TX: CALICO.

Yoo, S. J., & Huang, W. H. D. (2011). Comparison of web 2.0 technology acceptance level based on cultural differences. *Educational Technology & Society, 14*, 241–52.

Young, J. R. (2001). Does 'digital divide' rhetoric do more harm than good? *The Chronicle of Higher Education, 48*. Retrieved January 27 2016 from http://chronicle.com/article/Does-Digital-Divide-/3058

Zheng, B., & Warschauer, M. (2015). Participation, interaction, and academic achievement in an online discussion environment. *Computers & Education, 84*, 78–89.

Ziemke, K. (2012, November 7). What can #Twitter do for your students? Read our #HurricaneSandy adventure! [Blog post.] Retrieved January 27 2016 from https://literacyspark.wordpress.com/2012/11/07/what-can-twitter-do-for-your-students-read-our-hurricanesandy-adventure/

Index

Page numbers annotated with 'g' refer to glossary entries.